FRESH
BREAD
COMPANION

FRESH BREAD COMPANION

by Liz Clark

Interior Illustrations
Jane Lawrence

Cover Illustration
Lisa Adams

The Brick Tower Press ®
1230 Park Avenue, New York, NY 10128
Copyright © 2000
by Liz Clark

Clark, Liz
The Traditional Country Life Recipe Series:
Includes Index
ISBN 1-883283-11-6, softcover

Library of Congress Catalog Card
Number: 97-74017
First Edition, November 2000

TABLE OF CONTENTS

With Gratitude

For research and memories of bakeries a half century ago–from Keokuk to Joplin–Mary Beth Cahill, "Bud" Bloom, Anne Smith, Emmy Cortese and Jessie Hubbs. For taking my handwritten scribbles into the age of technology–Sandy Seabold and fellow author on the *Apple Companion*–Jill Vorbeck. For breaking down my recipes for the bread machine–Martha Johnstone and Betsy Colby. For reminiscences of the Wyatt and Peters families and old times on the Hilton Road–Louise Peters. Undying gratitude to all of the food professionals who have been willing to bake in my kitchen–Betsy Oppeneer, Nick Malgieri, Jill Van Cleave, Shirley Corriher, and Suzanne Corbett.

In Italy–Albertina, Pierangela and Maria Rosa. In France–the entire Arakelian family from Nick and Yevette to children and grandchildren, and in the south–the late Richard Olney and David and Nito Carpita. The Latin origins of the word "companion" mean "those with whom you break bread." May we all continue to do so....

"There is absolutely nothing that you can do wrong with bread, except kill the yeast!"

The deep-seated and ancient significance of bread goes beyond written history. We find threshing floors in prehistoric settlements and hieroglyphics devoted to harvesting on the walls of the tombs in ancient Egypt. As man turned to communal life and left the ways of hunting and gathering, his first agricultural act was to cultivate the wild grasses to produce the seed which was then threshed and ground into grits for gruel and rudimentary flour.

In the mysterious Bories–the domed stone-building village near Gordes in southeastern France, huge flat stone floors, created from a single rock are a central feature of the living areas. These threshing floors are adjacent to domed buildings whose walls contain charred baking ovens which must have been the communal bakeries for the settlements. Though their origins are lost in prehistory, these beehive-like buildings were actually used and inhabited well into this century.

The first breads were the flat breads common to every culture throughout the agricultural world. Risen or leavened breads probably came about quite by accident, as the wild, air-born yeasts settled on wet dough and fermented. People learned to save some of this fermented dough to be used in their next breads, thus creating the original "sour dough." In Italy, this saved dough is a "biga," in France a "levain," and it trekked across the western American continent in the 1850s as our now famous "sourdough."

Bread became central to cultures for their sustenance as meat was scarce and expensive to raise and difficult to keep. Flour could be milled and stored for baking during the lean months and bread became the focus of nourishment. "Give us this day our daily bread" is a line to which most of us give little thought as we routinely repeat it in the Christian ritual, yet it is one of the central requests of the Lord's prayer. The symbolic presence of bread in the Christian religion is seen in the host: bread and wine—body and blood of Christ. The cross slashed in the tops of loaves of bread served not just to vent the gases produced by the yeast as the bread was introduced to the oven, but as a benediction and a request for God to bless the loaves.

Long before utensils were introduced for "civilized" dining, bread or "trenchers" was used as a vehicle to convey food, often from communal pots, to the mouth—hence the term "trencherman." In most equatorial cultures today, some form of flat bread, be it chapatti, wonton, tortilla, or naan is still used, either as a wrapper or a utensil to carry food to the mouth. Since the post-war baby boomers began to travel internationally in the 1960s many of these ethnic, heretofore unknown breads have become main-stream American: witness fast-food pita sandwiches available in every plastic strip-mall drive-thru!

Tragically, just as our own country-farm loaves were prostituted in the name of progress into the awful white cotton commercial breads we see in supermarkets today, so were the ethnic breads of third-world cultures toned down to pale images of themselves as they were commercially mass-produced in this country. The average supermarket shopper has no sense of the true character of a pita found in even a Manhattan Syrian grocery of the 1960s. One of the few ways to appreciate what real bread tastes like is to bake your own. Nothing makes a house smell like "home" like the aroma of yeast bread in the oven. In fact, real estate agents often say that the best way to sell a house is to have bread baking when prospective buyers tour!

Bread baking is also one of the most satisfying, if not therapeutic, of all kitchen activities. As you begin to work with yeast and appreciate that the dough, like wine, is a living thing, ancient relationships are subliminally triggered. The hearth, round and central to the house, was dedicated to Hestia, the mother goddess in ancient Greece, and the only one of the Greek Pantheon never to be personified in mortal form. The grinding of flour and the baking of bread which transpired on this hearth were an act of worship to this spirit of hearth and home.

As civilization advanced and labor became more specialized, the miller and the baker became two of the most important craftsmen in the community. Chaucer's *Miller's Tale* gives us a bawdy, comic view of this very important member of medieval society. Farmers brought their grain to be ground into flour and the miller kept a share of the finished product in payment, selling it at profit to non-agricultural members of the community. From this practice emerged some of the earliest forms of commerce in modern western culture.

The community baker was central to the culinary life of western European villages well into the twentieth century. Until the advent of the free-standing commercially available range with a built-in oven, most cooking was done over an open hearth. Spit-roasted and kettle-stewed dishes were the day-to-day cuisine, and home baking was rare. All of the bread for a village was baked by the baker and bought fresh daily. The baker's oven was used by the villagers to roast and bake in the residual heat, once the bread was removed each day.

In France, families would carry their Sunday dinner in its baking dish to the village baker where it would be placed in the still-warm oven and retrieved following mass: hence such dishes as Leg of Lamb Boulanger—a roast leg of lamb on a gratin of potatoes "in the manner of the baker." Marcel Pagnol conveys to us the importance of the baker to the life of a community in his classic film, *La Femme du Boulanger*. When the baker's wife leaves him for a lover and he looses his will to bake, the entire community rallies to bring her back because they cannot exist without his bread.

In Russia, peasants always gathered to bless and bring good luck to a new house by carrying bread and salt as the first goods to cross the threshold. One of the most poignant and tragic reminders of the importance of bread to sustenance can be seen in Russia yet today. In St. Petersburg, at the museum of the cemetery where victims of the siege of Leningrad were buried in mass trenches, exhibits illustrate the events of the 900 Days. In a glass case on one wall, along with hundreds of photographs, a piece of dried black bread is mounted. This dark square measures little more than 2 or 3 inches across. It is the bread ration that was allotted to the population each day, and in most cases, the sole nutrition on which they survived Hitler's onslaught.

Bread and Memories

Liz's earliest memories of fresh bread are the loaves of country white bread made by her great aunts. Alice Wyatt and Alveretta Peters Wyatt were sisters-in-law and each, separately, wonderful bakers.

Uncle John and Alveretta lived on the Hilton Road, just down the hill, across the creek, and up the road from the farm where Liz was raised. Though, in retro-

spect, Liz realizes that they lived very frugally, as a child their farm impressed her with its riches. Rows of cherry trees lined the drive, canes laden with black and red raspberries weighed heavily against their support wires in the garden–feasts waiting for the picking on warm summer mornings. But best of all, there was Alveretta's homemade bread.

Alveretta usually baked early in order to avoid heating up the kitchen on summer days. Liz remembers the two rounded, golden loaves in their pans emerging from the old cast iron and enameled stove. The fragrance was like nothing else on earth–yeast, sugar, milk; pure Norman Rockwell. But best of all was Alveretta slicing into the still-warm loaves and allowing Liz to slather the heel with farm-churned butter which melted into the wonderful holes in the crumb, and then to eat it. At age 5 or 6 Liz could devour an entire loaf before the steam had ceased to rise from the last slice. Each year, for her birthday, Liz would receive a special delivery of two still-warm loaves for as long as Alveretta and Uncle John lived in the gray stucco farm house on the Hilton Road.

Aunt Alice, by contrast, lived in town. Though raised on the Hilton Road Place, she and her sister Caroline (Daisy) had moved into town and purchased a then-lovely Italianate brick house on High Street. The two maiden ladies operated the home as a rooming house, and Keokuk's bachelor Mayor Willmering lived there in Liz's childhood. Alice was another consummate baker, and though her loaves, like Alveretta's, stir memories, it was another yeast dough of hers which lives on most vividly in Liz's childhood flash-backs.

Halloween was, from earliest reflection, Liz's favorite holiday. Because she lived on the farm, trick-or-treating meant going to town and being led out around the neighborhood from Daisy's and Alice's, or from her Grandmother Clark's. No matter which neighborhood she was based in each year, the "Halloween Witch" always found Liz. The witch would knock mysteriously on the door, but by the time someone answered, she was gone. The only tell-tale sign of who had been there was a brown paper bag, twisted tightly at the top, and sometimes the witch would forget her broom! Inside the bag were still-warm sugared yeast doughnuts! To this day Liz finds all commercial doughnuts quite disgusting. Glazes and colored sprinkles are not her idea of what a doughnut should be. Only yeast doughnuts, fried in hot lard and shaken in granulated sugar will do–and preferably only at Halloween!

Daisy and Alice's house on High Street was only three blocks from Main Street and the then central business district of the 1940s and 1950s. Because they did not drive, Alice would walk downtown to pay her utility bills or make small purchases. The highlight of Liz's walks with her was the stroll past the bakery between 5th and 6th streets on the north side of Main. A spring-operated, green frame, screen door fronted on Main and the aromas which wafted out on a summer day were the most incredible yet unintentional advertising any business could have. Alice would often purchase a loaf of salt-rising bread and allow Liz the unbelievable luxury of a cream horn. In Liz's youth there was a proliferation of bakeries up and down Main Street. The largest and most commercial of them, Schouten's Bakery, made Donald Duck Bread! (A sliced white commercial loaf which licensed the Disney character.) The smaller more ethnic bakeries specialized in pastries and small-batch breads such as "Bohunk" (never considered an ethnic slur, but merely referring to the round shape of the loaf and its Eastern European origins), potato, and salt-rising loaves. It was rumored that the reason for the flavor of the bread from one bakery, which shall remain unnamed, was that the portly baker kneaded the batches of dough on his bare chest and belly!

Sadly, one by one, as the families retired or the bakers died, the Main Street bakeries were sold or closed. Today, only Stan's Pastry remains, a nostalgic reminder of mid-century Main Street.

Each summer during the 1940s and 1950s Liz's mother would pack Liz and her little brother into her green Plymouth coup (or later her black Kaiser sedan) and head diagonally across the state of Missouri to visit Grandmother and Grandfather Ruhl in their large white frame house on North Byers Street in Joplin. Grandmother Ruhl's flower beds against the back fence jutted up against the back of the neighborhood grocery store, easily accessible through the back gate. This was a daily source of penny candy and fresh, though commercial, bread for breakfast toast. Markwardts, a local Joplin bakery, marketed a loaf which they called "Butter and Egg Bread." Liz's mother would always stock up on several loaves to take home to Keokuk. Not until 30 years later, and countless sojourns in France, did Liz make the association that this "Butter and Egg Bread" was a sliced, commercial postwar adaptation of French Brioche!

Those first times abroad for Liz in the 1960s forever changed her approach to what real bread was all about. The Italian family where Liz lived as an exchange student in 1968 never served a meal without bread, freshly purchased from the village baker in Gemonio. Albertina herself did not bake the bread, as it was immediately accessible each morning. These were hearty, crusty loaves that had to be sliced with a serrated knife when they were brought to the table. The crust crunched as it was cut, revealing a network of large open holes in the slightly beige interior. The soft white bread, only good for wadding into balls for dining hall food fights during Liz's college days, had nothing in common with these loaves!

These northern Italian country loaves were slightly sour and the crust tore at the roof of your mouth. You did not butter the bread, but merely ate it alongside the meal, often wiping up any sauces remaining in a bowl or plate with torn pieces of the bread.

As Liz traveled around Italy with the other members of the group from the Experiment in International Living and their exchange siblings she encountered different breads in each region. The bread was normally placed on the table when you sat down and everyone nibbled at it with drinks while waiting for the meal. One vivid memory stands out for Liz. In Tuscany the bread is made without salt. Liz's companions from northern Lombardy sprinkled salt on the bread as they ate it!

Most meals during these student days were taken in family-run trattorias where there was usually no choice of menu, but you were served what had been cooked that day. Often the soup or the salad contained left-over bread or vegetables were stuffed or sprinkled with seasoned crumbs. Obviously the bread did not go to waste. "Pappa al Pomodoro," or tomato and bread soup, was an Italian cousin to the dish which both Liz's mother and her great Aunt Alice had regularly made with leftover bread and tomatoes and called "Stewed Tomatoes." (See page 21.)

Following her first experience living abroad, Liz returned to Europe almost yearly. In 1969 it was to Sicily, for archeological digs. It was at breakfast in the Catania Airport, while waiting for a return flight to Rome, that she encountered her first brioche. The plump, carmel-colored pillow with its little round head and pleated sides, was glazed with egg and sprinkled with pearl sugar. This seemed an unbelievable luxury to Liz who had only read about the seemingly complicated bread in her *Woman's Day Encyclopedia of Cookery*.

That same year, as Liz hopscotched up the continent, she arrived for a week in Paris, and at her step-father's suggestion, had her hotel concierge call a family whom her step-father had known through the French underground during World War II. Liz never used her hotel room again, but spent the rest of the week with the Arakelian family in the little village of Mery-sur-Oise just north of Paris. Her immersion in French food had begun. Like Albertina in Italy, Yevette was a gifted natural cook. Everything came fresh from the garden and from the market each day, and fresh bread was bought daily from the local Boulanger. Crusty baguettes that shattered when you tore them were served at breakfast with butter and preserves, and simply alongside lunch and dinner. Like Albertina, Yevette did not bake her bread at home–there was no necessity for it. Local bakers began their first offerings of the morning in the middle of the night. Fresh baguettes were purchased at 7:00 a.m. and brought home for breakfast.

By the time Liz returned home that fall, her taste buds were set for what was to be a life-long passion–the quest for real food–food that tasted of what it was, made with the freshest ingredients treated with respect.

Bread was the first order to come under attack. In the 1960s only ethnic bakeries

in major cities were producing any breads which even bore a faint resemblance to the daily breads of the Europeans with whom Liz had lived. Most supermarket bread was of the white cotton "insulation" variety, unfit for human consumption after exposure to what real bread was about. Sadly, Liz's great aunts who had made the wonderful farmhouse loaves of her childhood had passed-on, and Liz's mother, though a good cook, had never taken an interest in baking bread on a regular basis.

The assault began! When Liz returned to Keokuk to teach elementary art in the 1960s she moved into the house at the farm where she had lived as a child. The house was vacant and the last tenants had owned their kitchen appliances and had taken them with them, necessitating Liz's first purchase of a kitchen! From the Sears and Roebuck Catalog she ordered a fashionable, avocado green, double oven stove and matching refrigerator.

Though she hungered for good bread, like so many who are daunted by the time element after reading a recipe containing yeast, Liz seldom tackled bread-baking except on a Saturday or Sunday. Her *Women's Day Encyclopedia of Cookery* had, for its time, a fairly thorough bread section, and a volume of James Beard's *Menus for Entertaining*, which she had permanently borrowed from her mother's library, contained a milk-based loaf which sounded similar to Alveretta's farm loaves of twenty years before.

Liz's first loaf of bread, like those of so many virgin bakers, was a flop! She used Beard's recipe, and as she now realizes, added her yeast to the scalded milk before it had sufficiently cooled. As Liz now tells bread baking cooking class students, "There is absolutely nothing that you can do wrong with bread, except kill the yeast!" If she did not completely kill her yeast with her first loaf, she certainly permanently disabled it! The loaf resembled the shape and size of your average brick!

After this first humiliating experience, it was a while before Liz tackled yeast again. But soon enough, cravings won out, and the Fleishman's packet once again came down from the cabinet. This time a bit more careful reading of the directions and more attention to the temperature of her liquid produced an adequate, if not prize-winning, loaf. The yeasty flavor of this still-warm bread slathered with butter was reward enough for the time spent. Still, time seemed like the element that could not be varied.

One weekday evening when bread yearnings got the better of her, Liz mixed up a batch of dough and set it aside for its first rise. By the time she had punched the dough down and shaped the loaves the time was edging close to midnight. Knowing she had to get up early the next morning a panic grabbed her. Which was more important: her bread or her sleep? With a sudden flash of inspiration she looked at her glamorous, avocado green, double oven stove with its oven timers—a timed bake cycle which would turn itself on and shut itself off. In went the loaves, in their pans, to the cold oven. She set the timers to allow the loaves to rise in the oven and then have the oven turn itself on, bake the loaves, and shut itself off—all while she slept!

Viola! The next morning, fresh baked bread! Admittedly, these first over-night loaves were not perfect. Adjustments had to be made for the rising time while the oven preheated, and for the baking time as the oven cooled down. Soon, however, remarkably good basic loaves were being pulled from Liz's oven at 6:30 a.m.

Attempts at sticky cinnamon rolls and basic caraway rye loaves followed, but Liz stuck fairly close to the farm-style loaves of her childhood for her first few years of baking. She did learn one very important lesson during this time—watch the expiration date on your yeast packet and, better yet, keep your yeast refrigerated! She also learned that it was far more economical to buy the jars of yeast if you are going to do any amount of baking than to pay the price for the individual 3-packs. She now purchases her yeast from co-ops or healthfood stores by the pound.

In 1970-71, Liz returned to graduate school for a year, after first spending the summer in western Europe and the British Isles. She bought a Porsche at the factory in Stuttgart, and for the first time had access to the backroads and country villages which today comprise her destinations. Here she found some of the first truly rustic breads which today make up the majority of her repertoire. These were hearty loaves with marvelous crusts. They were not of a uniform shape, and often had floury crusts. Stone-ground flours and a variety of additions, nuts, onions, coarse grains, fruits and herbs made each loaf an individual. The loaves differed from town to town and baker to baker. Liz and her friend Susan Batchelder, who traveled with her that summer, would often picnic at noon and save their money for a nice restaurant meal in the evenings.

Those roadside picnics usually included regional cheeses and sausages or patés, fresh vegetables and fruits, a bottle of the local wine, and of course, a loaf of bread from the local baker. Throughout the Loire Valley and Brittany and Normandy each village brought a new cheese and a new bread. No two loaves were the same, anymore than the cheeses were the same. Each loaf seemed more interesting than the last. That summer's drive through the French countryside was the equivalent of a graduate course in bread.

Liz had never seen loaves like these rustic country ones. No one that she was aware of in New York or Chicago was attempting to bake such breads. French bakeries in Boston or New York specialized in pastry-cream filled Napoleons and pretty royal icing petite fours, but not hearty country French breads.

When Liz returned from graduate school the following year she purchased the run-down twenty room rooming house where she lives and runs her cooking school and restaurant today. She occasionally baked her overnight oven-timed breads, but spent most of her time hiring workmen and superintending the renovation of the house. After living for a year and a half at her mother's while the house had to be completely gutted, Liz finally returned to her basically remodeled house. She cooked and entertained constantly. Then she finally realized by 1976 that the investment which she had made in the house could not be supported on a teacher's salary.

In November of 1976, Liz ran an ad in the local paper offering her services for catering private parties in her home. The timing was right, as the foodie trend was just hitting its stride. People had traveled abroad and restaurants on both coasts were beginning to offer regional French and Italian food to their clientele. It was no longer the tyranny of the "Continental" restaurant.

When Liz opened her restaurant in 1976, she served popovers for the bread to accompany her dinners. These elegant, puffy quick breads took her about 45 minutes from start to finish, and she could make them while proceeding with the other courses on the menu. Though people loved the popovers, Liz did find that, especially on a Saturday, when she felt she had the time, if she baked her basic French loaves people almost made a meal off of the bread. Soon she had requests from dinner customers 40 or 50 miles away to simply bake bread for them. They were willing to drive to Keokuk to pick it up, and happy to pay her asking price–$8.00 for 6 loaves! Finally Liz realized that between her bread and her coffee–freshly ground dark roast beans, still a rarity in most places–she could almost have gotten away with carry-in fast food for the main course, and no one would have noticed!

The yeast breads had become a staple on the dinner table, but Liz had to find a way to conquer the time element, while teaching all day, before coming home to cook and open the door to the paying customers at 7:00 p.m.

Once you are on a first name basis with yeast you realize that you don't have to hold its hand while it rises. Once the dough is set, placed in an oiled bowl, and covered with a clean linen towel, it takes on a life of its own. You can be doing your thing, while, like an exuberant teenager, it does its thing!

Liz found that she could come home from school on her lunch hour, proof her yeast, knead the dough in a heavy duty stand mixer with a dough hook, turn the dough out into an oiled bowl, cover it and put it in a draft free corner of the kitchen to rise while she went back to her teaching job for the afternoon.

When she came home at 4, she would punch down the dough, shape the loaves, and leave them to rise while the oven preheated. Suddenly, fresh bread–great bread–was possible every day, with a minimum of fuss and no baby-sitting the rising dough.

Though she has since retired from her teaching job and spends her time either chained to her stove or traveling, this is still Liz's basic philosophy where rising dough is concerned–"Love it and leave it." The leavening will take care of itself. Liz does offer one word of caution, however. Don't be too cavalier when grabbing a towel to cover the bowl of dough. If you use a terry cloth towel, you'll wish you hadn't! Unless you want to take a toothbrush to clean it up, you might as well throw the towel away! Be sure to use a clean linen or cotton tea towel.

About Stone-Ground Flours

Much of the appeal and full-bodied flavor of artesianal breads comes from the incorporation of stone-ground flours in their dough. Though a variety of these flours is available through most supermarkets, the pleasure of seeking out small mills who still grind flour in limited batches (and sell their products) can serve as a creative spring-board for a batch of bread. As well as whole wheat, rye and corn meals, you may find cracked wheat and bran cereals, and even stone-ground hominy grits.

Because these flours and grains usually contain the germ and the hull, their nutritional value is far superior to flours purchased in supermarkets. So is their taste! The fresh, nutty flavor of a stone-ground loaf leaves commercial breads sadly lacking by comparison. The complexity and layers of flavor in this type of bread allows you to begin to understand the primal, religious significance in which bread has been seen since prehistory.

Special handling is required in order to get the most from your mill purchases. Because they are ground in small batches, these flours are definitely more expensive than ordinary commercial flours, but you do not need inordinate amounts to transform a batch of bread from mundane to transcendental. A ten-pound bag of stone-ground whole wheat flour can, if properly stored, last the average "once-a-week baker" for up to six months.

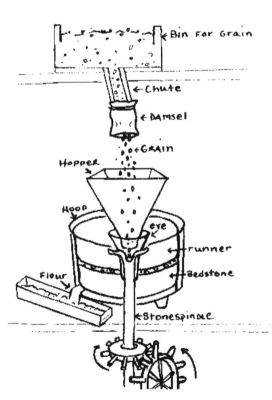

Since these flours contain no preservatives and have the hull and germ in them, they can turn rancid or attract insects very quickly. As soon as you get them home, divide the flours into gallon zip lock bags, label and date them and refrigerate. Do not store them in the paper bags they come in, as they will quickly absorb any off-flavors in your refrigerator. If the ten-pound bag is going to last you a year, freeze part of it. Bring the flour to room temperature before baking, so as not to slow down yeast development when setting your dough.

Once you are comfortable with baking these types of breads, you'll find yourself mixing flours and additives such as cereals and wheat germ; grains such as barley and rice, fruits, nuts, herbs, and vegetables. A visit to a mill may inspire an all new loaf, based on a local sorghum, molasses, or regional honey, sitting there waiting for your serendipitous discovery.

Please try these flours. Make a weekend road trip or a busman's holiday to a mill you've heard about. Buy the flours and experiment with combinations, creating your own signature loaves. Most mills will happily ship to you if traveling to them is impossible.

Not only will you reward yourself with some of the tastiest, most nutritious breads you can eat, but you will be encouraging the perpetuation of a trade as old as civilization.

SOURDOUGH STARTER

 INGREDIENTS

2 cups of warm water
2 tablespoons of yeast
2 cups of unbleached flour

(1) Mix water, yeast, and flour in a medium-sized, non-reactive (enamel) bowl.
(2) Cover bowl with plastic wrap; secure with rubber band. Let ferment at room temperature for 4 days.
(3) Every time you use 1 cup of the Starter, add 1 cup of water and 1 cup of flour.

NOTE: Sourdough Starter will keep indefinately if fed once a week and refrigerated between uses. Bring to room temperature each time you use it.

PAPPA AL POMODORO

(1) In a large enameled Dutch oven, heat the olive oil over medium heat until it begins to move or "smile" on the bottom of the pan.

(2) Add the onions and cook, stirring constantly until the onions are soft, but have not taken on any color.

(3) Stir in the garlic, bay leaves, thyme, and oregano.

(4) Continue stirring for one minute, or until you can smell the garlic but it has not taken on any color.

(5) Add the chicken stock, tomatoes, and reserved cubed bread.

(6) Reduce heat to simmer and cook, stirring occasionally for 30 minutes or until bread and tomatoes have softened and blended together into a thick porridge.

(7) Ladle the soup into bowls and serve topped with freshly grated pepper and Parmesan cheese.

NOTE: Once you have taken the time to make good bread it should not go to waste. Liz encountered this Italian version of what her mother and great aunts referred to as "Stewed Tomatoes" when she first lived as an exchange student in Italy in the 1960s.

☞ INGREDIENTS

2-3 cups of stale homemade country loaves, diced, reserved

1/2 cup of extra-virgin olive oil

3 large yellow onions, peeled and chopped

4 large garlic cloves, minced

3 bay leaves

1 teaspoon of dried thyme (1 tablespoon fresh)

2 teaspoons of dried oregano (2 tablespoons fresh)

3 quarts of chicken stock

8 large tomatoes peeled, seeded and chopped

freshly ground pepper

freshly grated Parmesan cheese for garnish

SERVES 8

RUSTIC BAGUETTES

(1) Proof yeast in the 1/2 cup of warm water with the tablespoon of sugar.

(2) Whisk with a wire whisk to aerate and dissolve the yeast. After about 5 minutes the mixture should appear quite foamy if the yeast is working.

(3) Whisk in the 2 remaining cups of warm water and the tablespoon of sea salt.

(4) Add the 1/2 cup of whole wheat flour and 5 cups of the unbleached or all-purpose flour.

(5) Stir to combine. If dough is extremely wet add another cup of flour.

(6) Place in the bowl of a heavy duty electric mixer fitted with a dough hook and knead, adding a bit more flour if necessary, until the dough cleans the sides of the bowl. Do not be alarmed if the dough does not clump and form a ball around the dough hook. This is meant to be an extremely wet dough.

(7) Coat a large mixing bowl with cooking oil and turn dough into it.

(8) Push the dough around in the bowl, coating the ball of dough completely with oil.

(9) Cover with a linen cloth and set aside in a draft-free place until dough has doubled in bulk. The rising time will depend on room temperature and humidity conditions, but normally this will take one to two hours.

(10) When the dough has risen turn it out on a well floured surface, such as a pastry cloth, and pat out into a circle about 14 inches wide and 3/4-inch thick.

(11) With an extremely sharp knife, cut the dough into six pie-shaped wedges.

(12) Turn in all of the corners of a wedge, and rolling from the center point toward you, loosely roll up the wedge to form a cylinder.

(13) Holding the cylinder of dough vertically, gently stretch the dough (like milking a cow) into an even rope of dough about 14 inches long.

(14) Place the dough on a cookie sheet that has been sprayed with non-stick baking spray and coated with cornmeal.

(15) Proceed in exactly the same way with the remaining five wedges of dough. You should have three equal loaves of bread on each of two cookie sheets.

(16) Cover each sheet with a linen towel and set aside to rise again until doubled.

Preheat the oven to 400° F.

(17) Position the oven shelves one third of the way from the top and one third of the way from the bottom of the oven. (If your oven is large enough to hold the cookie sheets side by side, position the shelf in the center of the oven.)

(18) When the loaves have doubled in size, slash each one diagonally several times down the length of the loaf. (Five or six slashes is about right.)

(19) Place the pans in the preheated oven and set the timer for 15 minutes.

(20) Alternate the pans at the end of 15 minutes so that the top of the loaves will brown evenly.

(21) Bake for another 15 minutes or until the loaves are browned and sound hollow when tapped. Remove the loaves from the oven and cool on wire racks.

NOTE: Liz uses one half cup of stone-ground whole wheat flour in combination with all-purpose or unbleached flour to achieve the country texture and flavor that she is looking for in this bread. A good, wet dough helps to develop the crust which is so desirable in this loaf.

INGREDIENTS

1 tablespoon of dry yeast
1/2 cup of warm water (not more than 115° F.) + 2 additional cups of warm water
1 tablespoon of sugar
1 tablespoon of sea salt
1/2 cup of stone-ground whole wheat flour
5-7 cups of unbleached or all-purpose flour + flour for shaping loaves
cooking oil to coat bowl
non-stick spray and cornmeal for coating baking pans

NOTE: "This is the bread we've looked for all over the country!" Jan Filkins exclaimed in our Winter Salads and Crusty Breads cooking class!" Indeed, this is the bread that most people are searching for when they think of those full flavored French loaves that once upon a time awakened them as to what real bread was all about. Maybe it was a student European excursion, or lunch in an American Bistro with a backet of artesenal, stone-ground loaves, but wherever they experienced it, no one ever forgets the primal appeal of the most basic of foods.

MAKES 6 BAGUETTES

SOURDOUGH FRENCH LOAVES

(1) Proof yeast in 1/2 cup of warm water.

(2) Stir in the additional 2 cups of water and the Sourdough Starter.

(3) Add sea salt and sugar and stir to dissolve.

(4) Stir in 5 cups of unbleached flour and any of the remaining flour to make a stiff but workable dough.

(5) Continue to knead until dough is smooth (about 15 minutes by hand, or until the dough cleans the sides of the bowl, if using a mixer with a dough hook).

(6) Place the dough in an oiled bowl, turning to coat, and cover with a cloth.

(7) Place in a warm spot and allow to rise until doubled in bulk.

(8) Turn dough out on a floured surface and shape into six baguette sized loaves.

(9) Place loaves on 2 baking sheets that have been greased and sprinkled with cornmeal.

(10) Cover and allow to rise again until doubled.

Preheat the oven to 400° F.

(11) Place racks in the middle of the oven.

(12) Make diagonal slashes in the top of each loaf and brush with water.

(13) Bake for 10 minutes, remove from oven and brush with water again.

(14) Alternate trays on shelves when replacing.

(15) Repeat twice, for a total of 30 minutes baking time. Remove loaves from oven and cool on racks.

⊕ INGREDIENTS

1 tablespoon of dry yeast
1/2 cup of warm water (not
   more than 115° F.) + 2 additional cups of warm water
1 cup of active Sourdough
   Starter (see page 20)
1 tablespoon of sugar
1 tablespoon of sea salt
5-8 cups of unbleached flour
cornmeal for baking sheets

MAKES 6 LOAVES

ITALIAN LOAVES

(1) Proof yeast in 1/2 cup of warm water.
(2) Add malt syrup, sourdough starter, salt, additional water, and milk.
(3) Stir to dissolve malt syrup, salt, and sugar
(4) Add 5 cups of unbleached flour.
(5) Stir to combine. Stir in the olive oil.
(6) In a mixing bowl fitted with a dough hook, knead dough until it cleans the sides of the bowl. Add additional flour if dough is too sticky.
(7) Oil a large mixing bowl, place dough in bowl and turn to coat.
(8) Cover with a towel and set aside to rise until doubled in bulk (at least 1 hour).
(9) Punch dough down and divide in half.
(10) Shape into 2 long free-form loaves.
(11) Place on a baking sheet lightly brushed with olive oil and sprinkled with cornmeal.
(12) Cover and allow to rise until doubled (at least 30 minutes).
(13) Slash loaves.

Preheat the oven to 400° F.

(14) Place an empty roasting pan on the lowest shelf of the oven while it is preheating.
(15) Wearing an oven mitt, pour 1 cup of water into the roasting pan. (Be very careful, as the steam can burn you!!)
(16) Place the baking sheet with the 2 loaves on the middle shelf of the oven.
(17) Bake for 30 minutes, or until water has evaporated and loaves sound hollow when tapped. Cool on a rack.

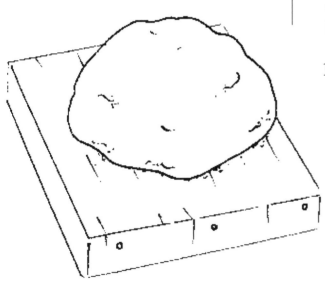

1 tablespoon of dry yeast
1/2 cup of warm water (not more than 115° F.)
1 tablespoon of malt syrup or extract (available from a brewers' supplier or health food store)
1 cup of active Sourdough Starter (see page 20)
1 tablespoon of salt
1 tablespoon of sugar
1 cup of warm water (not more than 115° F.)
1 cup of warm milk (not more than 115° F.)
5-8 cups of unbleached flour
extra-virgin olive oil and cornmeal for baking sheet

MAKES 2 LONG LOAVES

ROSEMARY/CURRANT BREAD

(1) In the bowl of an electric mixer fitted with a dough hook, proof the yeast with 1/2 cup of warm water and the sugar.

(2) When the yeast is foaming, add the remaining 2 cups of warm water and the salt.

(3) Stir to dissolve the salt.

(4) Add the 2 cups of whole wheat flour and 3 cups of the unbleached flour.

(5) Stir to mix, then knead with the dough hook, adding as much additional flour as necessary for dough to form a smooth mass which cleans the side of the bowl.

(6) Knead in the currants and rosemary. The mixture may need a little more flour at this point.

(7) Place the dough in a large bowl coated with oil and turn to coat.

(8) Cover the bowl with a clean linen towel and place in a warm spot to rise until doubled in bulk.

(9) Turn out on a floured surface and pat into a circle about 1-inch thick.

(10) Cut into 4 pieces and pinch the corners together to form a round loaf.

(11) Coat tops with flour and place loaves, pinched-side down, on cookie sheets which have been coated with cornmeal.

(12) Cover. Allow to rise again for about 1 hour.

Preheat the oven to 400° F.

(13) Slash tops of loaves.

(14) Place loaves in oven and bake for 30-35 minutes, or until they sound hollow when tapped. Cool on racks.

NOTE: All over France you will find breads of this type served with the cheese course. Their robust texture is perfect with any cheese, but the most heavenly marriage is with the superb goat cheeses (chèvre) of Provence. We are beginning to produce some excellent goat cheeses in this country*. Make this bread the next time you find one!

*Fantome Farms, RR #1, Ridgeway, Wisconsin 53582 produces what Liz considers to be a world-class chèvre. Call Anne and she will ship to you. (608-924-1266)

⚘ INGREDIENTS

2 tablespoons of dry yeast
1/2 cup of warm water (not
  more than 115° F.)
1 tablespoon of sugar
2 tablespoons of sea salt
2 cups of warm water (not more
  than 115° F.)
2 cups of stone-ground whole
  wheat flour
3-5 cups of unbleached flour
1 cup of dried currants, covered
  with boiling water and
  plumped, cooled
4, 4-inch branches of rosemary,
  leaves stripped and minced
non-stick spray or cornmeal for
  coating cookie sheets

MAKES 4 LOAVES

FERMENTED CRACKED WHEAT AND HAZELNUT LOAVES

(1) In the bowl of an electric mixer fitted with the dough hook proof the yeast in the 1/2 cup of warm water with the sugar.

(2) Add the remaining two cups of warm water and the salt and whisk to combine.

(3) Stir in the cracked wheat cereal.

(4) Add the whole wheat flour and three cups of the unbleached flour.

(5) Coarsely chop the hazelnuts and add to the dough.

(6) Knead with dough hook adding as much of the remaining flour as necessary for dough to form a smooth mass and clean the side of the bowl.

(7) Place the dough in a large bowl coated with oil and turn to coat.

(8) Cover the bowl with a clean towel and put in a warm place to rise until doubled in bulk.

(9) Turn out on a floured surface and pat into a circle about 1-inch thick.

(10) Cut into 4 pieces and pinch the corners together to form a round loaf.

(11) Coat tops with flour and place loaves, pinched-side down, on cookie sheets which have been coated with cornmeal.

(12) Cover with clean towels.

(13) Allow to rise again for about 1 hour.

Preheat the oven to 400° F.

(14) Slash tops of loaves. Place loaves in oven and bake for 30 minutes, reversing sheets after 15 minutes.

(15) Bake until loaves sound hollow when tapped. Cool on racks.

⏚ INGREDIENTS

24 hours before starting bread:
2 cups of cracked wheat cereal*
boiling water to cover

(1) Place the cracked wheat cereal in a glass or ceramic bowl and pour boiling water over it to cover.
(2) Leave standing at room temperature, uncovered, for 24 hours.

2 tablespoons of dry yeast
1/2 cup of warm water (not more than 115° F.) + 2 cups of additional warm water
1 tablespoon of sugar
1 tablespoon of salt
reserved cracked wheat cereal (above)
2 cups of stone-ground Nauvoo or other whole wheat flour
3-5 cups of unbleached flour
1 cup of toasted hazelnuts, skins rubbed off
non-stick baking spray or cornmeal for cookie sheets

NOTE: Covering cracked wheat cereal with boiling water and allowing it to ferment at room temperature for twenty-four hours will produce a slightly sour flavor, reminiscent of a country sourdough loaf, in this rich, autumn-flavored bread. The hazelnuts add a wonderful crunch which makes toast from this bread the perfect accompaniment to a cheese platter.

*Available from Nauvoo Mill and Bakery, 1530 Mulholland Street, Nauvoo, IL 62354 (217-453-6734) www.visitnauvoo.org

MAKES 4 LOAVES

BARLEY AND ONION
COUNTRY LOAVES

(1) In the bowl of an electric mixer fitted with the dough hook, proof the yeast in the 1/2 cup of warm water with the sugar.

(2) Add the salt to the yeast mixture and stir until dissolved.

(3) Pour in the 2 cups of additional warm water.

(4) Add 2 cups of the whole wheat flour and 4 cups of the unbleached flour and stir. If the mixture is quite sticky, add more unbleached flour.

(5) Knead with the dough hook adding as much of the remaining flour as necessary for the mixture to form a ball and clean the sides of the bowl.

(6) Add barley and onion to the mixture.

(7) Place the dough in a large bowl coated with cooking oil and turn to coat.

(8) Cover with a clean linen towel and place in a warm draft-free place to rise until double in bulk.

(9) Turn dough out on a floured surface and pat out into a circle about 1-inch thick.

(10) Cut into 2 pieces and pinch the corners together to form a round loaf.

(11) Coat tops with flour and place loaves, pinched-side down, on cookie sheets which have been coated with cornmeal.

(12) Cover loaves with linen towels and allow to rise again for about 1 hour.

Preheat the oven to 400° F.

(13) Slash tops of loaves. Place loaves in oven and bake for about 30-35 minutes, or until they sound hollow when tapped. Cool on racks.

*NOTE: Hearty barley adds a nutty tex-
ture, as well as flavor and nutrition,
to these robust peasant-type loaves.
The added savor of onion makes
them the perfect accompaniment to
full-flavored wintry stews. Picture
Sunday night supper in front of a
cozy fire.*

 INGREDIENTS

1 tablespoon of dry yeast
1/2 cup of warm water (not
   more than 115° F.) + 2 cups
   of additional warm water
1 tablespoon of sugar
1 tablespoon of salt
2 cups of stone-ground whole
   wheat flour
4-5 cups of unbleached flour
1 cup of quick-cooking barley,
   prepared according to package
   directions, cooled and
   reserved
2 medium yellow onions,
   peeled, diced, and reserved
cornmeal for cookie sheets

MAKES 2 LOAVES

BLACK OLIVE & WALNUT BREAD
WITH THYME

(1) In the bowl of an electric mixer fitted with a dough hook, proof the yeast in the 1/2 cup of warm water with the sugar.

(2) When the yeast is foaming, add the Sourdough Starter, the remaining 1 cup of warm water, and the salt.

(3) Stir to dissolve salt.

(4) Add the 2 cups of whole wheat flour and 3 cups of the unbleached flour.

(5) Stir to mix, then knead with the dough hook, adding as much additional flour as necessary for dough to form a smooth mass which cleans the side of the bowl.

(6) Knead in the olives, walnuts, thyme and olive oil. The mixture may need a little more flour at this point.

(7) Place the dough in a large bowl coated with olive oil and turn to coat.

(8) Cover the bowl with a clean towel and place in a warm spot to rise until doubled in bulk.

(9) Turn out on a floured surface and pat out into a circle about 1-inch thick.

(10) Cut into 4 pieces and pinch the corners together to form a round loaf.

(11) Coat tops with flour and place loaves, pinched-side down, on cookie sheets which have been coated with cornmeal.

(12) Cover. Allow to rise again for about 1 hour.

Preheat the oven to 400° F.

(13) Slash tops of loaves.

(14) Place loaves in oven and bake for 30-35 minutes, or until they sound hollow when tapped. Cool on racks.

NOTE: *Liz took these loaves to her friend Richard Olney when she went to visit him one summer while she was teaching cooking classes in the South of France. He liked the bread well enough to simply trade her the bread he had on hand for the remainder of her loaves when they had finished lunch!*

🍂 INGREDIENTS

1 tablespoon of dry yeast
1/2 cup of warm water (not more than 115° F.)
1 tablespoon of sugar
1 cup of active Sourdough Starter (see page 20)
1 tablespoon of salt
1 cup of warm water (not more than 115° F.)
2 cups of stone-ground whole wheat flour
3-5 cups of unbleached flour
1/2 cup of pitted Mediterranean black olives (Kalamata or Niçoise)
1 cup of chopped English walnuts
2 tablespoons of minced fresh thyme (2 teaspoons dried)
1/2 cup of extra-virgin olive oil
cornmeal for cookie sheets

MAKES 4 LOAVES

ONION/DILL BREAD

(1) In the bowl of an electric mixer fitted with a dough hook, proof the yeast with 1/2 cup of warm water and the sugar.

(2) When the yeast is foaming, add the remaining 2 cups of warm water and the salt.

(3) Stir to dissolve the salt.

(4) Add the 2 cups of whole wheat flour and 3 cups of the unbleached flour.

(5) Stir to mix, then knead with the dough hook, adding as much additional flour as necessary for dough to form a smooth mass which cleans the side of the bowl.

(6) Knead in the onions, dill weed, and dill seed. The mixture may need a little more flour at this point.

(7) Place the dough in a large bowl coated with oil and turn to coat.

(8) Cover the bowl with a clean towel and place in a warm spot to rise until doubled in bulk.

(9) Turn out on a floured surface and pat into a circle about 1-inch thick.

(10) Cut into 4 pieces and pinch the corners together to form a round loaf.

(11) Coat tops with flour and place loaves, pinched-side down, on cookie sheets which have been coated with cornmeal.

(12) Cover. Allow to rise again for about 1 hour.

Preheat the oven to 400° F.

(13) Slash tops of loaves. Place loaves in oven and bake for 30-35 minutes, or until they sound hollow when tapped. Cool on racks.

NOTE: *Of all the breads which Liz makes, this has always been Barb Harrison's favorite. Huge handsful of Barb's dill come in to Liz in the spring and are transformed into loaves of this earthy bread. Try a slice warm, just from the oven, with the butter melting into it.*

☞ INGREDIENTS

2 tablespoons of dry yeast
1/2 cup of warm water (not more than 115° F.)
1 tablespoon of sugar
2 tablespoons of sea salt
2 cups of warm water (not more than 115° F.)
2 cups of stone-ground whole wheat flour
3-5 cups of unbleached flour
2 medium, yellow onions, peeled and diced
1/2 cup of chopped fresh dill
1 tablespoon of dill seed
cornmeal for cookie sheets

MAKES 4 LOAVES

BURGUNDIAN COUNTRY LOAVES / BLACK SESAME AND YELLOW MUSTARD SEED

(1) In the bowl of a heavy duty mixer, fitted with the dough hook, proof the yeast with 1/2 cup of warm water and the sugar. Whisk to aerate and mix thoroughly.

(2) When the yeast is foaming, whisk in the remaining water and the sea salt.

(3) Add the toasted seeds and the whole wheat and rye flours and stir thoroughly.

(4) Add 4 cups of the unbleached flour.

(5) Place the mixer bowl on the stand and begin to mix on low. Watch the consistency of the dough–it must be moist but not runny. Add more flour as necessary, until a still moist, but manageable dough is achieved.

(6) Remove the dough to a large bowl that has been brushed with vegetable oil.

(7) Cover the bowl with a linen towel and place in a warm spot to rise until doubled in bulk.

(8) Turn the dough out onto a floured surface and pat out into a circle about 1 1/2 inches thick.

(9) With a sharp knife, cut the dough into 4 equal wedges.

(10) Pull the corners of each wedge of dough to the center (like a baby's diaper). With your fingers, gingerly dimple the bottom of the loaf to eliminate any seams.

(11) Spray two light-colored baking sheets with non-stick spray and sprinkle with cornmeal.

(12) Gently turn the loaves over and place, seam side down, on the baking sheets.

(13) Cover again with linen towels and allow to rise for about 1/2 hour.

(14) Slash the top of the loaves.

Preheat the oven to 400° F.

(15) Position oven shelves equidistant from the top and bottom of the oven.

(16) Place loaves in the preheated oven and set timer for 15 minutes.

(17) After 15 minutes, reverse baking

sheets and continue to bake for another 15-20 minutes, or until loaves sound hollow when rapped with your knuckle.

(18) Remove loaves form oven and cool on wire racks.

NOTE: *In the autumn of 1997, Liz was having lunch on the terrace of the Jardin du Ramparts, one of Beaune's most creative restaurants, while she waited for her room to be readied at the nearby Hotel de la Poste. After traveling throughout France doing research for her bread book, one more basket of bread seemed redundant. But as she waited between courses, one roll in the basket cried out to be sampled. Breakinginto it, Liz discovered a combination of ingredients which, in all of her experimentation, she had never considered- in the classical Burgundian dough of light wheat and rye flours was a mixture of black sesame seeds andwhole yeallow mustard seeds. A phenomenal taste combination. Liz returned to New York, told her publisher John Colby that room had to be left in the manuscript for this particular bread, then went home to Keokuk to perfect it.*

☞ INGREDIENTS

1 tablespoon of yeast
1/2 cup of warm water (not more than 115° F.)
1 1/2 tablespoons of sea salt
2 cups of warm water (not more than 115° F.)
2 tablespoons of black sesame seeds*, toasted
2 tablespoons of yellow mustard seeds, toasted
1/2 cup of stone-ground whole wheat flour
1/2 cup of stone-ground rye flour
5-6 cups of unbleached flour
1 tablespoon of vegetable oil
non-stick spray and cornmeal for baking sheets

*Black sesame seeds are available at Oriental markets.

MAKES 4 LOAVES

WALNUT BREAD
WITH NAUVOO FLOUR

(1) Proof the yeast in the warm water in a large bowl.
(2) Add the sourdough starter, sugar, salt, olive oil, and milk.
(3) Stir with a wooden spoon to mix thoroughly.
(4) In another large bowl, sift together the 2 cups of whole wheat flour and five cups of the unbleached flour.
(5) Make a well in the center of the flour and pour in the starter mixture.
(6) Knead well to incorporate the flour, adding some of the remaining 3 cups of unbleached flour if dough is too sticky.
(7) Work the walnuts and onion into the dough until they are completely incorporated.
(8) Place the dough in a greased bowl, cover with a cloth and allow to rise until doubled in bulk.
(9) When dough has doubled, punch down and divide into quarters.
(10) Shape into four round loaves.
(11) Roll tops of loaves in flour to coat, and place on a greased baking sheet coated with cornmeal.
(12) Let rise for one hour.
(13) Slash an "X" in the top of each loaf, then bake in a preheated 400° F. oven for 45 minutes, or until loaves sound hollow when tapped.

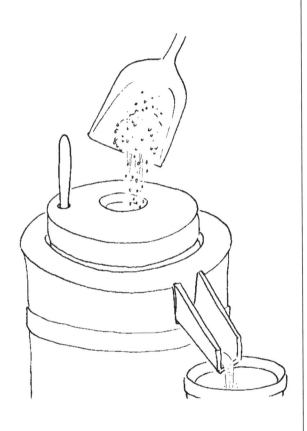

INGREDIENTS

2 tablespoons of dry yeast
1/2 cup of warm water (not
    more than 115° F.)
1 cup of active Sourdough
    Starter (see page 20)
2 tablespoons of sugar
1 tablespoon of salt
1/2 cup of olive oil
2 cups of warm milk
2 cups of stone-ground whole
    wheat flour*
8 cups of unbleached flour
1 cup of chopped walnuts
1 large yellow onion, chopped
cornmeal for baking sheets

*Available from Nauvoo Mill and
    Bakery, 1530 Mulholland
    Street, Nauvoo, IL 62354
    (217-453-6734)
    www.visitnauvoo.org

MAKES 4 SMALL LOAVES

HONEY, SUNFLOWER SEED &
CRACKED WHEAT LOAF

(1) Proof the yeast in the 1/2 cup of warm water with the honey.

(2) When yeast is foaming, stir in the remaining water, salt, olive oil, and cracked wheat cereal.

(3) Add the whole wheat flour and three cups of the unbleached flour.

(4) Add the sunflower seeds and knead the dough with the hook of an electric mixer. If dough is sticky, add more unbleached flour. When the dough is the proper consistency, it will clean the sides of the mixer bowl.

(5) Place dough in a large bowl coated with olive oil and cover with a towel.

(6) Place in a warm spot and allow to rise until doubled in bulk (about 1 hour).

(7) Turn dough out on a floured surface and pat out into a circle about 1-inch thick.

(8) Cut into 4 pieces and pinch the corners together to form a round loaf.

(9) Place loaves, pinched-side down, on cookie sheets which have been coated with cornmeal.

(10) Cover. Allow to rise again for about 1 hour.

Preheat the oven to 400° F.

(11) Slash tops of loaves.

(12) Bake for 30 minutes or until loaves sound hollow when tapped.

(13) Remove from oven and cool on racks.

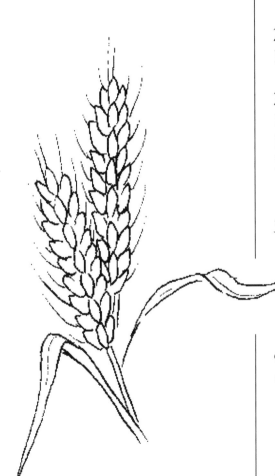

INGREDIENTS

2 tablespoons of dry yeast
1/2 cup of warm water (not more than 115° F.)
2 tablespoons of honey
1 tablespoon of salt
1 tablespoon of olive oil
1/2 cup of cracked wheat cereal* soaked in boiling water to make 1 cup
3 cups of stone-ground whole wheat flour
3-5 cups of unbleached flour
1 cup of roasted, hulled sunflower seeds (unsalted)
cornmeal for cookie sheets

*Available from Nauvoo Mill and Bakery, 1530 Mulholland Street, Nauvoo, IL 62354 (217-453-6734) www.visitnauvoo.org

MAKES 4 LOAVES

COUNTRY LOAVES/BACON

(1) In the bowl of an electric mixer fitted with the dough hook, proof the yeast in the 1/2 cup of warm water with the sugar.

(2) While the yeast is proofing, sauté the bacon in a large enameled cast iron skillet over medium-high heat.

(3) When bacon has crisped, remove it to a paper towel and set aside.

(4) Reserve bacon fat and allow to cool.

(5) When fat has cooled to where you may touch the bottom of the skillet with your hand, add 1/2 cup water to the bacon fat.

(6) Return the skillet to the stove and heat the fat and water over low heat, scraping the bottom of the skillet with a wooden spatula to incorporate every bit of the residue.

(7) Pour this mixture into a 2-cup Pyrex measure and add enough warm water to equal 2 cups.

Check the temperature of the liquid to be sure that it is no more than 115° F.

(8) Add the salt to the yeast mixture and stir until dissolved. Pour in the bacon fat and water. Stir again.

(9) Add 5 cups of the flour and stir.

(10) Stir in the reserved sautéed bacon. If the mixture is quite sticky, add more flour.

(11) Knead with the dough hook, adding as much of the remaining flour as necessary for the mixture to form a ball and clean the sides of the bowl.

(12) Place the dough in a large bowl coated with cooking oil and turn to coat.

(13) Cover with a clean linen towel and place in a warm draft-free place to rise until doubled in bulk.

(14) Turn dough out on a floured surface and pat out into a circle about 1-inch thick.
(15) Cut into 4 pieces and pinch the corners together to form a round loaf.
(16) Coat tops with flour and place loaves, pinched-side down, on cookie sheets which have been coated with cornmeal.
(17) Cover loaves with linen towels and allow to rise again for about 1 hour.

Preheat the oven to 400° F.

(18) Slash tops of loaves.
(19) Place loaves in oven and bake for about 30 minutes, or until they sound hollow when tapped. Cool on racks.

✒ INGREDIENTS

1 tablespoon of dry yeast
1/2 cup of warm water (not more than 115° F.)
1 tablespoon of sugar
1/2 pound of good quality bacon, chopped
1/2 cup of water + water to make 2 cups of liquid
1 teaspoon of salt
5-7 cups of unbleached flour
cornmeal for cookie sheets

MAKES 4 LOAVES

CHEDDAR, APPLE, THYME
SOURDOUGH BREAD

(1) In the bowl of an electric mixer fitted with the dough hook, proof the yeast in the 1/2 cup of warm water with the sugar.

(2) Add the Sourdough Starter.

(3) When the yeast is foaming, add the salt and the remaining 2 cups of warm water.

(4) Stir to dissolve the salt.

(5) Add the whole wheat flour and 3 cups of the unbleached flour.

(6) Stir to mix.

(7) Add the apples, cheese, and thyme, then knead with the dough hook to form a smooth mass which cleans the sides of the bowl.

(8) Place the dough in a large bowl coated with cooking oil and turn to coat.

(9) Cover with a clean linen towel and place in a warm, draft-free place to rise until doubled in bulk.

(10) Turn dough out on a floured surface and pat out into a circle about 1-inch thick.

(11) Cut into 4 pieces and pinch the corners together to form a round loaf.

(12) Coat tops with flour and place loaves, pinched-side down on baking sheets which have been sprayed with non-stick spray and sprinkled with cornmeal.

(13) Cover loaves with linen towels and allow to rise again for about 1 hour.

Preheat the oven to 400° F.

(14) Slash tops of loaves.

(15) Place loaves in oven and bake for about 30 minutes or until they sound hollow when tapped. Cool on racks.

NOTE: *When the cooking class group from Willow Hollow in Lincoln, Nebraska came for an intensive weekend of classes with Liz, we made this bread in the morning "Autumn Harvest" class. That evening we sliced one of the remaining loaves paper thin and made melba toast to go with our appetizer paté. A real hit!*

MAKES 4 LOAVES

🍞 INGREDIENTS

1 tablespoon of dry yeast
1/2 cup of warm water (not more than 115° F.)
1 tablespoon of sugar
1 cup of active Sourdough Starter (see page 20)
1 tablespoon of salt
2 cups of warm water (not more than 115° F.)
1 1/2 cups of stone-ground whole wheat flour
4-6 cups of unbleached flour
2 firm red apples such as Jonathans or Cortlands, cored but not peeled, and cut into 1/2-inch dice
1 cup of shredded Cheddar cheese
3 tablespoons of minced fresh thyme (1 teaspoon dried)
non-stick baking spray and cornmeal for coating baking sheets

PAIN DECORÉ

(1) Proof yeast in 1/2 cup of warm water.

(2) Stir in the additional 2 cups of water.

(3) Add sea salt and sugar and stir to dissolve.

(4) Stir in 1 cup of whole wheat flour plus enough unbleached flour to make a stiff but workable dough.

(5) Continue to knead until dough is smooth (about 15 minutes by hand or until the dough cleans the sides of the bowl, if using a mixer with a dough hook).

(6) Place the dough in an oiled bowl, turning to coat, and cover with a cloth.

(7) Place in a warm spot and allow to rise until doubled in bulk.

Shaping Loaf:

(8) When dough has risen, turn out onto a floured cloth and pat out into a circle about 3/4-inch thick.

(9) With a sharp knife, cut out a heart shape about 12 inches wide.

(10) From the remaining dough shape flowers, stems, leaves and any other decorations you desire.

(11) Dust heavily with flour and place the loaf on a baking sheet coated with cornmeal and cover with a linen towel.

(12) Set aside to rise until doubled. (The decoration will adhere as the bread rises.)

Preheat the oven to 400° F.

(13) Place the baking pan with the heart loaf on the center shelf of the preheated oven.

(14) Bake for 35-40 minutes, or until loaf is golden and sounds hollow when tapped. Remove from oven and cool loaf on a baking rack.

NOTE: Any dough left after shaping the heart and decorating it may be kneaded together and shaped into a loaf. Bake in a loaf pan coated with non-stick baking spray and cornmeal. Use for sandwich bread.

NOTE: Halfway up the hill on the way to the Pilgrimage Cathedral in the Burgundian town of Autun, and ancient bakery stands on a corner. For years Liz has been taken by the stunning loaves of bread that filled their bakery windows. Fanciful animals, figures of peasant boys and girls, and huge country loaves decorated with sheaves of wheat, bunches of flowers or fruits intrigued her year after year. This decorative Valentine loaf was inspired by these works of art.

INGREDIENTS

VALENTINE HEART LOAF

1 tablespoon of dry yeast
1/2 cup of warm water (not more than 115° F.)
2 cups of warm water (not more than 115° F.)
1 tablespoon of sugar
1 tablespoon of sea salt
1 cup of stone-ground whole wheat flour
5-6 cups of unbleached flour
1 tablespoon of vegetable oil
flour for dusting

MAKES 1 HEART LOAF

POMPE DE NOEL

(1) In the bowl of an electric mixer fitted with the dough hook, proof yeast in the 1/2 cup of warm water with the tablespoon of sugar.

(2) When the yeast is foaming add the salt and the remaining 2 cups of warm water.

(3) Stir to dissolve the salt.

(4) Add the whole wheat flour, sugar, orange zest, orange flower water, olive oil, and 3 cups of the unbleached flour.

(5) Stir to mix, then knead with the dough hook, adding as much of the remaining flour as necessary for the dough to form a smooth mass which cleans the sides of the bowl.

(6) Place the dough in a large bowl coated with cooking oil and turn to coat.

(7) Cover with a clean linen towel and place in a warm place to rise until doubled in bulk.

(8) Turn dough out on a floured surface and pat into a circle about 1-inch thick.

(9) Cut into 4 pieces and pinch the corners together to form a round loaf.

(10) Coat tops with flour and place loaves, pinched-side down on baking sheets which have been sprayed with non-stick spray and sprinkled with cornmeal.

(11) Cover loaves with linen towels and allow to rise again for about 1 hour.

Preheat the oven to 400° F.

(12) Slash tops of loaves. Place loaves in oven and bake for about 30 minutes or until they sound hollow when tapped. Cool on racks.

NOTE: *No Christmas table in Provence is complete without this bread. Every bakery throughout the region prepares it, and for many of the Provencale homes this is one bread which will be handmade. Grated orange peel and orange flower water are necessities. An orange zester makes the zest a simple addition, and orange flower water is easily procured from specialty bake shops or Oriental markets.*

⌖ INGREDIENTS

2 tablespoons of yeast*
1/2 cup of warm water (not
    more than 115° F.)
1 tablespoon of sugar
1 tablespoon of salt
2 cups of warm water
1/2 cup of whole wheat flour
1/2 cup of sugar
zest of 1 orange
3 tablespoons of orange flower
    water
1/2 cup of extra-virgin olive oil
6-7 cups of unbleached flour
non-stick spray and cornmeal
    for baking sheets

**1 tablespoon of regular yeast + 1 tablespoon brewer's yeast. Liz likes to add one tablespoon of brewer's yeast to the dough to increase the "yeast" aroma and flavor.*

MAKES 4 LOAVES

PRUNE AND ALMOND WHOLE WHEAT LOAVES

(1) In the bowl of an electric mixer fitted with the dough hook, proof the yeast in the 1/2 cup of warm water with the sugar.

(2) Whisk thoroughly with a wire whisk to dissolve and aerate the yeast.

(3) When the yeast is foaming, add the sea salt and the remaining 2 cups of warm water.

(4) Whisk to dissolve the salt.

(5) Add the whole wheat flour and three cups of the unbleached flour.

(6) Stir to mix, then knead with the dough hook, adding as much of the remaining flour as necessary in order to form a smooth, but very moist, dough which cleans the sides of the bowl and somewhat clings to the dough hook.

(7) Knead in the chopped prunes and almonds.

(8) Transfer the dough to a large mixing bowl which you have coated with the cooking oil.

(9) Turn the dough so that it is completely coated with oil.

(10) Cover with a clean linen towel and place in a warm, draft-free place to rise until doubled in bulk (about 1-2 hours).

(11) Turn the dough out onto a well floured surface, such as a pastry cloth, and pat out into a circle about 13 inches or 14 inches wide and 1-inch thick.

(12) With a sharp knife, cut the dough into 4 equal wedges.

(13) Pull the corners of the wedges together and pinch them to seal.

(14) With your fingertips lightly dimple the bottom of each loaf until the seams disappear. This will also accomplish the task of gently adhering a good coating of flour from the work surface to the top of the loaf.

(15) Turn the loaves and place them seam-sides down on two cookie sheets which have been sprayed with non-stick spray and sprinkled with cornmeal.

(16) Cover the loaves with linen towels and set aside to rise again until doubled (about one hour).

Preheat the oven to 400° F.

(17) Position oven racks one third of the way from the top and one third of the way from the bottom of the oven.
(18) Slash the tops of the loaves in a tick-tack-toe pattern.
(19) Place loaves in the oven and bake for 15 minutes. Alternate pans and bake for another 15 to 20 minutes, or until the loaves sound hollow when tapped. Remove from oven and cool on racks.

NOTE: *Liz is constantly experimenting with breads to accompany a cheese tray—normally her favorite way to end a meal. Round, slightly uneven, country loaves, filled with fruits, nuts, olives or herbs often fill the bill. Their floured tops and wonderful crusts fairly scream "handmade." Try these loaves toasted with cheeses such as Brie and Gruyère and a bit of sweet butter. The next day, how about cinnamon toast with a morning cappuccino?*

INGREDIENTS

1 tablespoon of dry yeast
1/2 cup of warm water (not more than 115° F.)
1 tablespoon of sugar
1 tablespoon of sea salt
2 cups of warm water (not more than 115° F.)
2 cups of stone-ground whole wheat flour
3-4 cups of unbleached flour, plus flour for shaping loaves
1/2 cup of soft pitted prunes, chopped
1/2 cup of toasted whole almonds
oil for bowl
non-stick baking spray and cornmeal for coating baking sheets

MAKES 4 ROUND LOAVES

RAISIN, SUNFLOWER SEED RYE LOAF

(1) Proof the yeast in the half cup of warm water with sugar.

(2) When yeast is forming, stir in the remaining water, salt and the rye flour. Mix thoroughly.

(3) Add the unbleached flour until a stiff dough is formed*.

(4) Stir in the raisins, cornmeal, and the sunflower seeds.

(5) Knead with the dough hook of a heavy-duty mixer until dough stretches from the sides of the bowl in long, elastic strands. (The dough will resemble chocolate chip cookie dough at this point.) Do not add too much unbleached flour, or loaves will be leaden.

(6) Place dough in an oiled bowl and turn to coat.

(7) Cover with a linen towel. Allow to rise until doubled in bulk.

(8) Turn dough out on a floured cloth.

(9) Shape dough into two round loaves and coat the tops with flour.

(10) Place loaves on baking sheets that have been sprayed with non-stick baking spray and sprinkled with cornmeal.

(11) Cover with linen towels and allow to rise for about 1 hour, or until doubled in size.

Preheat the oven to 400° F.

(12) Slash the tops of the loaves.

(13) Place the loaves on the center shelf of the oven and bake for 30 minutes or until loaves sound hollow when tapped. Cool on wire racks.

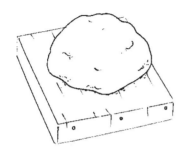

Rye bread dough is notoriously sticky. Do not over-react and add so much flour that your bread becomes heavy and tough. The dough is most easily handled by using a curved plastic bowl scraper.

NOTE: *This hearty peasant-style loaf is "almost dessert" as Barb Norman remarked in the cooking class. It is wonderful toasted for breakfast and spread with butter and apple butter.*

☙ INGREDIENTS

2 tablespoons of dry yeast
1/2 cup of warm water (not more than 115° F.)
1 tablespoon of sugar
1 tablespoon of salt (if using salted sunflower seeds, omit salt)
2 cups of warm water (not more than 115° F.)
1 1/2 cups of stone-ground rye flour
1/2 cup of cornmeal
5-7 cups of unbleached flour
1 cup of raisins, plumped in boiling water and drained
1/2 cup of toasted sunflower seeds
non-stick spray and cornmeal for baking sheets

MAKES 2 LOAVES

CORNMEAL BREAD

(1) Cover the stone-ground cornmeal with boiling water and stir and leave to sit overnight at room temperature.

(2) Fry bacon until crisp. Drain and reserve bacon fat.

(3) In the bowl of a heavy duty mixer, fitted with the dough hook, proof the yeast with the warm water and the sugar. Whisk to aerate and mix thoroughly.

(4) When the yeast is foaming, whisk in the remaining cup of water and the sea salt.

(5) Stir in the softened cornmeal, which will add considerable moisture.

(6) Add 4 cups of the all-purpose flour and stir thoroughly.

(7) Add the cooled bacon fat and reserved bacon and the cheddar cheese.

(8) Place the mixer bowl on the stand and begin to mix on low. Watch the consistency of the dough—it must be moist but not runny. Add more flour as necessary, until a still moist, but manageable dough is achieved.

(9) Remove the dough to a large bowl that has been brushed with vegetable oil, turn to coat, cover with a linen towel, and place in a warm spot to rise until doubled in bulk.

(10) Turn the dough out onto a floured surface and pat out into a circle about 1 1/2 inches thick.

(11) With a sharp knife, cut the dough into 4 equal wedges.

(12) Pull the corners of the dough to the center (like a baby's diaper).

(13) With your fingers, gingerly dimple the bottom of the loaf to eliminate any seams.

(14) Spray two light-colored baking sheets with non-stick spray and sprinkle with cornmeal.

(15) Gently turn the loaves over and place, seam-side down, on the baking sheets.

(16) Cover again with linen towels and allow to rise for about 1/2 hour.

(17) Slash the tops of the loaves.

Preheat the oven to 400° F.

(18) Position oven shelves equidistant from the top and bottom of the oven.
(19) Place loaves in the preheated oven and set timer for 15 minutes.
(20) After 15 minutes, reverse baking sheets and continue to bake for another 15-20 minutes, or until loaves sound hollow when rapped with your knuckle.
(21) Remove loaves form oven and cool on wire racks.

NOTE: *When Liz had a group of childhood friends for lunch, following the death of the mother of close friend Mary Younkin McMurray, she served the sort of comfort food appropriate to a cold winter day, chicken/rice/shiitake mushroom soup, and crusty loaves of this hearty bread. From the day of the luncheon on, good friend Judy Petry Walrath has hounded Liz for the date of the book's publication so that she could get the recipe! Here, for Judy, Mary, and everyone else who raved about the loaves, is the recipe!*

☙ INGREDIENTS

2 cups of stone-ground cornmeal
boiling water
1/2 pound of good quality bacon
2 tablespoons of yeast
1/2 cup of warm water (not more than 115° F.)
2 tablespoons of sugar
1 tablespoon of sea salt
1 cup of warm water (not more than 115° F.)
4-6 cups of all-purpose flour
1 pound of extra-sharp Cheddar cheese, shredded
vegetable oil
non-stick spray for baking sheets
cornmeal for baking sheets

MAKES 4 LOAVES

HERBED LOAVES

(1) In the bowl of a heavy duty mixer fitted with the dough hook, proof the yeast with the 1/2 cup of warm water and the sugar. (Whisking to mix and dissolve the yeast helps to accelerate the proofing.)

(2) Add the salt when the yeast is foaming.

(3) Whisk again to thoroughly dissolve the salt.

(4) Add the 2 remaining cups of water and stir well.

(5) Mix in the flour. Using 5 cups of flour adding more, as necessary, to make a soft but compact ball of dough which cleans the sides of the mixer bowl when processed with the dough hook. (Depending on the humidity and the moisture content of your flour, this can take anywhere from 5 to 7 cups of flour.)

(6) Oil a bowl and turn the dough out into it, turning to coat the ball of dough with the oil.

(7) Cover with a linen towel and put in a draft-free place to rise until doubled in bulk.

(8) Turn the dough out onto a floured surface and pat out into a circle about 1-inch thick.

(9) Cut the dough circle in half.

(10) Spread each half with the Herb Butter (recipe follows). (see note on page 60)

(11) Roll up into a cylinder, turning in the ends to completely enclose the butter.

(12) Spray two 10x5-inch loaf pans with non-stick cooking spray.

(13) Place the dough seam-side down in the pans.

(14) Cover with linen towels and allow to double in bulk.

(15) Place the dough in a large bowl coated with oil and turn to coat.

(16) Cover the bowl with a clean linen towel and place in a warm spot to rise until doubled in bulk.

(17) Turn out on a floured surface.

Preheat the oven to 400° F.

(18) Slash the top of each loaf 4 or 5 times.
(19) Place the loaves on the center shelf of the oven and bake for 40-45 minutes, or until golden and hollow-sounding when tapped. Remove the loaves from the oven, turn out on a wire rack to cool.

NOTE: This flavorful and versatile bread dough may be shaped in any way that suits you, as we proved in the "Summer Fruits and Vegetables" cooking class. Loaf pans of varying sizes, or free-form country loaves work equally well with this herb-butter filled yeasty dough. Do not be limited by the herbs which Liz uses in the butter. Your personal preferences and what your garden grows will all work wonderfully.

☞ INGREDIENTS

1 tablespoon of yeast
1/2 cup of warm water (not more than 115° F.)
1 tablespoon of sugar
1 tablespoon of sea salt
2 cups of warm water (not more than 115° F.)
1/2 cup of stone-ground whole wheat flour
5-6 cups of unbleached flour
non-stick spray for loaf pans

MAKES 2 LOAVES

HERB BUTTER

(1) Place softened butter in a small bowl.
(2) Add herbs and cayenne pepper.
(3) With a fork, cream together until well combined.
(4) Use butter to coat flattened bread dough before shaping loaves.

NOTE: *This herb combination is not engraved in stone. Any fresh herbs which you have available, in combinations pleasing to you, may be substituted.*

☙ INGREDIENTS

1 stick of lightly salted butter (4 ounces)
4 garlic cloves, peeled and finely minced
1 tablespoon of fresh rosemary, finely chopped
1 tablespoon of fresh thyme, finely chopped
2 tablespoons of fresh basil, finely chopped
1/2 teaspoon of cayenne pepper

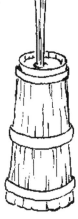

APPLESAUCE, WHOLE WHEAT BREAD

(1) Proof yeast in the 1/2 cup of warm water.
(2) Mix the apple sauce and the remaining cup of warm water together.
(3) Add to the yeast mixture and stir.
(4) Mix in the whole wheat flour, bran flour, and 3 cups of the unbleached flour.
(5) Stir to combine.
(6) Knead with the dough hook to form a smooth mass which cleans the sides of the bowl.
(7) Place the dough in a large bowl coated with cooking oil and turn to coat.
(8) Cover with a clean linen towel and place in a warm, draft-free place to rise until doubled in bulk.
(9) Turn dough out on a floured surface and pat out into a circle about 1-inch thick.
(10) Cut into 4 pieces and pinch the corners together to form a round loaf.
(11) Coat tops with flour and place loaves, pinched-side down on baking sheets which have been sprayed with non-stick spray and sprinkled with cornmeal.
(12) Cover loaves with linen towels and allow to rise again for about 1 hour.

Preheat the oven to 400° F.

(14) Slash tops of loaves.
(15) Place loaves in oven and bake for about 30 minutes or until they sound hollow when tapped. Cool on racks.

INGREDIENTS

1 tablespoon of dry yeast
1/2 cup of warm water (not more than 115° F.) + 2 additional cups of warm water
1 cup of fresh apple sauce
1 cup of warm water (not more than 115° F.)
1 tablespoon of salt
2 cups of Nauvoo* or other stone-ground whole wheat flour
1 cup of bran flour*
3-5 cups of unbleached flour
non-stick spray and cornmeal for baking sheets

*Available from Nauvoo Mill and Bakery, 1530 Mulholland Street, Nauvoo, IL 62354 (217-453-6734) www.visitnauvoo.org

MAKES 4 LOAVES

PESTO-FILLED LOAVES

(1) In the bowl of a heavy-duty mixer fitted with the dough hook, proof the yeast with the warm water and sugar. (Whisking to mix and dissolve the yeast helps to accelerate the proofing.)
(2) Add the salt when yeast is foaming.
(3) Whisk again to thoroughly dissolve the salt.
(4) Add the remaining 2 cups of warm water and stir well.
(5) Mix in the flour.
(6) Use 5 cups of flour and add more, as necessary, to make a soft but compact ball of dough which cleans the sides of the mixer bowl when processed with the dough hook. (Depending on the humidity and the moisture content of your flour, this can take anywhere from 5 to 7 cups of flour.)
(7) Oil a bowl and turn the dough out into it, turning to coat the ball of dough with the oil.
(8) Cover with a linen towel and put in a draft-free place to rise until doubled in bulk.
(9) Turn the dough out onto a floured surface and pat out into a circle about 1-inch thick.
(10) Cut the dough circle in half.
(11) Spread each half with the Pesto.
(12) Roll up into a cylinder, turning in the ends to completely enclose the pesto.
(13) Spray two 10x5-inch loaf pans with non-stick cooking spray.
(14) Place the dough, seam-side down, in the pans.
(15) Cover with linen towels and allow to double in bulk.

NOTE: *Free form loaves may be baked by placing the rolled cylinders on oiled cookie sheets coated with cornmeal. Be sure that ends are tucked under and sealed.*

Preheat the oven to 400° F.

(16) Slash tops of each loaf 4 or 5 times.
(17) Place the loaves on the center shelf of the oven and bake for 40-45 minutes, or until golden and hollow-sounding when tapped. Remove the loaves from the oven, turn out on a wire rack to cool.

NOTE: *Italian in flavor, this savory loaf is a perfect accompaniment to any country-style soup. It needs no butter, thanks to the olive oil in the pesto, which permeates the bread as it bakes. This flavorful and versatile bread dough may be shaped in any way that suits you. Loaf pans of varying sizes, or free-form country loaves work equally well with this pesto-filled yeasty dough.*

INGREDIENTS

1 recipe Basil Pesto, reserved (see box)
1 tablespoon of dry yeast
1/2 cup of warm water (not more than 115° F.)
1 tablespoon of sugar
1 tablespoon of sea salt
2 cups of warm water (not more than 115° F.)
1/2 cup of stone-ground whole wheat flour
5-6 cups of unbleached flour

MAKES 2 LOAVES

BASIL PESTO

INGREDIENTS

1 large bunch of basil, stems removed
6 large garlic cloves, chopped
1 cup of pine nuts, toasted in a 300° F. oven for 15 minutes
1 cup of freshly grated Parmesan cheese
1/2-3/4 cup of olive oil
freshly grated black pepper to taste

(1) Place basil, garlic, pine nuts and Parmesan in the container of a food processor fitted with the steel blade.
(2) Process until finely ground.
(3) With motor running, add olive oil in a steady stream until a fairly liquid paste is achieved.
(4) Add freshly grated pepper to taste.

MAKES ABOUT 3 CUPS

BRAIDED LOAVES

(1) Proof yeast in 1/2 cup of warm water.
(2) Stir in the additional 2 cups of water.
(3) Add sea salt and sugar and stir to dissolve.
(4) Stir in 5 cups of unbleached flour and any of the remaining flour to make a stiff but workable dough.
(5) Continue to knead until dough is smooth (about 15 minutes by hand, or until the dough cleans the sides of the bowl, if using a mixer with a dough hook).
(6) Place the dough in an oiled bowl, turning to coat, and cover with a cloth.
(7) Place in a warm spot and allow to rise until doubled in bulk.
(8) Turn dough out on a floured surface and divide into 6 pieces.
(9) Braid 3 pieces together and twist into a circle.
(10) Braid 3 pieces together tucking under ends and leave long. Allow to rise a second time.

GLAZE

1 extra-large egg beaten with 1 table-spoon of water
sesame seeds
poppy seeds

(1) Brush one loaf with egg wash and sprinkle with toasted sesame seeds.
(2) Brush other loaf with egg wash and sprinkle with poppy seeds.
(3) Place on cookie sheets sprayed with non-stick spray and coated with cornmeal.

Preheat the oven to 400° F.

(4) Bake in 400° F. oven about 30 minutes, or until they sound hollow when tapped. Cool on wire racks.

NOTE: *These are the loaves that will convince people that you are a baker! They are the kind that you pay premium prices for in artesenal bakers in most cities. Liz always includes one or two on any buffet where she is doing mountains of bread–they are the ones people "ooh" and "ahh" over!*

☞ INGREDIENTS

1 tablespoon of dry yeast
1/2 cup of warm water (not more than 115° F.) + 2 additional cups of warm water
1 tablespoon of sugar
1 tablespoon of sea salt
5-8 cups of unbleached or all-purpose flour + flour for shaping loaves
cooking oil to coat bowl
non-stick spray and cornmeal for coating baking pans

Glaze (see page 64)

MAKES 2 LOAVES

SEEDED BRAID LOAVES

(1) Proof yeast in a mixing bowl in the 1/2 cup of warm water and the sugar.

(2) When the yeast is foaming, stir in the 2 remaining cups of warm water, the salt, and 5 cups of the flour.

(3) Add seed mixture.

(4) Knead the mixture with the dough hook of an electric mixer, adding in more flour if necessary.

(5) When dough cleans the side of the bowl turn it out into an oiled bowl and cover with a towel.

(6) Place in a warm spot to rise until doubled in bulk (about 1 hour).

(7) Turn dough out on a flat surface and pat out into a circle about 1/2-inch thick.

(8) Cut circle into 6 wedges.

(9) Roll wedges into a cylinder and stretch between the palms of your hands to a length of about 2 feet.

(10) To form braids, overlap three pieces of dough in the center and braid to both ends.

(11) Pinch ends together. A braid may be twisted into a wreath and the ends pinched to join them.

(12) Place loaves on cookie sheets coated with cornmeal.

(13) Cover. Allow to rise for about 1 hour.

Preheat the oven to 400° F.

(14) Glaze braids with the egg white and water mixture and sprinkle with the 2 tablespoons of remaining seed mixture.

(15) Bake loaves for 35 to 40 minutes, or until they sound hollow when tapped.

INGREDIENTS

2 tablespoons of dry yeast
1/2 cup of warm water (not
    more than 115° F.) + 2 addi-
    tional cups of warm water
1 tablespoon of sugar
1 tablespoon of sea salt
5-7 cups of unbleached flour
2 tablespoons of mixed seed and
    cheese salad seasoning (avail-
    able in the spice section of
    the supermarket).

(for glazing)

1 egg white mixed with 1 table-
    spoon of cold water
2 tablespoons mixed seed and
    cheese salad seasoning

MAKES 2 BRAIDS OR
WREATHS

DARK POPPY SEED, RYE LOAVES
WITH APPLE

(1) In the bowl of an electric mixer fitted with the dough hook, proof the yeast in the 1/2 cup of warm water with the sugar.

(2) Stir with a wire whisk and allow to foam.

(3) Stir in the additional 2 cups of warm water and the sea salt.

(4) Whisk to dissolve the salt.

(5) Add the 2 cups of whole wheat flour, 2 cups rye flour, and 2 cups of the unbleached flour. Add enough of the remaining flour to make a stiff but workable dough.

(6) Add 1/4 cup of the toasted poppy seeds, cocoa powder and dissolved coffee. Add the diced apples.

(7) Knead with the dough hook until the mixture forms a ball and cleans the sides of the bowl.

(8) Place the dough in an oiled bowl and turn to coat.

(9) Cover with a linen towel.

(10) Place in a warm spot and allow to rise until doubled in bulk.

(11) Turn dough out on a floured surface and divide into 6 pieces.

(12) Braid 3 of the pieces together and twist into a circle.

(13) Braid 3 pieces together and leave long.

(14) Allow to rise a second time.

GLAZE

1 extra-large egg beaten with 1 tablespoon of water
1/4 cup of poppy seeds

(15) Brush loaves with egg wash and sprinkle with toasted poppy seeds.

Preheat the oven to 400° F.

(16) Place loaves on cookie sheets sprayed with non-stick spray and sprinkle with cornmeal.

(17) Bake for 30-35 minutes or until loaves sound hollow when tapped. Cool on wire racks.

NOTE: *Reminiscent of the black breads of Russia, the secret to this showy, delightful bread is powdered cocoa and instant coffee granules. They give the rich loaves their characteristic mahogany color and slightly bitter taste. Braiding bread dough is no more difficult than the pigtails of childhood. Start by crossing the three strips of dough in the center and braiding outward. This will assure you of a more even finish at each end.*

✿ INGREDIENTS

1 tablespoon of dry yeast
1/2 cup of warm water (not
    more than 115° F.)
1 tablespoon of sugar
1 tablespoon of sea salt
2 cups of warm water (not more
    than 115° F.)
2 cups of stone-ground whole
    wheat flour
2 cups of stone-ground rye flour
2-3 cups of unbleached flour
1/4 cup of poppy seeds
3 tablespoons of unsweetened
    cocoa powder
3 tablespoons of instant coffee,
    dissolved in 2 tablespoons of
    warm water
2 small Jonathan apples, cored
    but not peeled, and cut into
    1/2-inch dice
Glaze (see page 68)

MAKES 2 LOAVES

SWEET POTATO, CARAWAY RYE BRAIDS

(1) In the bowl of an electric mixer fitted with the dough hook, proof the yeast in the 1/2 cup of warm water with the sugar.

(2) Stir with a wire whisk to dissolve.

(3) When the mixture is foaming add the remaining two cups of warm water and the sea salt.

(4) Whisk to dissolve the salt.

(5) Stir in the whole wheat flour, rye flour and 3 cups of the unbleached flour.

(6) Place the bowl on the mixer and knead with the dough hook until well combined.

(7) Add the reserved mashed sweet potato, caraway seeds, and enough additional flour to make a workable dough.

(8) This dough will not clean the sides of the bowl and will more resemble cookie dough than the usual bread dough. Knead 3 to 4 minutes.

(9) Transfer dough to an oiled mixing bowl, turn to coat thoroughly, and cover with a linen towel.

(10) Set aside in a warm, draft-free place to rise until doubled in bulk (about 1 hour).

(11) Turn dough out onto a floured surface and pat out into a circle about 16 inches wide and 1-inch thick.

(12) Cut the dough into six equal wedges with a sharp knife.

(13) With floured hands, roll the wedges into cylinders and stretch into even ropes about 16 inches long.

(14) Braid three of the ropes by crossing them in the middle and braiding toward each end.

(15) Tuck the ends under and press to seal.

(16) Place the braid diagonally on a large cookie sheet which has been sprayed with non-stick spray and sprinkled with cornmeal.

(17) Repeat with the remaining three ropes of dough.

(18) Cover each loaf with a linen towel and place in a warm place to rise until doubled.

GLAZE

1 extra-large egg beaten with 1 tablespoon of water
2 tablespoons of caraway seeds

(19) Brush loaves with egg wash and sprinkle with caraway seeds.

Preheat the oven to 400° F.

(20) Position oven racks one third of the way from the top and one third of the way from the bottom of the oven.
(21) Place loaves in the oven and bake for 15 minutes.
(22) Switch pans and continue to bake for 20 to 30 minutes or until loaves are golden and sound hollow when tapped. Remove from oven and cool on wire racks.

☞ INGREDIENTS

2 medium sweet potatoes (or substitute yams) baked for about 1 hour in a 400° F. oven, peeled and mashed (reserved)
1 tablespoon of dry yeast
1/2 cup of warm water (not more than 115° F.)
1 tablespoon of sugar
1 tablespoon of sea salt
2 cups of warm water (not more than 115° F.)
1 cup of stone-ground whole wheat flour
2 cups of stone-ground rye flour
3-4 cups of unbleached flour, more if needed
1 tablespoon of caraway seeds
oil for bowl
non-stick cooking spray and cornmeal for baking sheet
Glaze (see adjacent column)

MAKES 2 LARGE BRAIDS

TOMATO, OLIVE, AND ROSEMARY
FOCACCIA

(1) In the bowl of an electric mixer fitted with the dough hook, proof the yeast in the 1/2 cup of warm water with sugar.

(2) Add the remaining water, salt, and olive oil.

(3) Stir in enough of the flour to form a stiff dough.

(4) Knead with the dough hook until the dough forms a ball and cleans the sides of the bowl.

(5) Place the dough in a bowl that has been coated with olive oil.

(6) Turn dough and cover with a linen towel.

(7) Allow to rise until doubled in bulk.

(8) Turn dough out on a floured cloth.

(9) Pat out into a large rectangle.

Preheat the oven to 400° F.

(10) Brush two 12x18-inch heavy baking sheets with olive oil.

(11) Sprinkle with cornmeal.

(12) Cut dough in half and press each half out to fit each of the baking pans.

(13) Brush each baking sheet of focaccia with the extra-virgin olive oil.

(14) Spread the chopped tomatoes and olives over the focaccia.

(15) Stud each loaf with half of the rosemary sprigs and sprinkle with the sea salt.

(16) Place the baking sheets on the center shelves of the preheated oven.

(17) Bake for about 30 minutes, reversing sheets halfway through the baking.

(18) Remove pans from oven and cool on wire racks. Cut into squares.

NOTE: *Focaccia is an almost pizza-like loaf, which may be topped with onion, garlic, anchovies, or other vegetables and herbs native to the Mediterranean. Its close relation on the French side of the Riviera is the similar fougasse. This is a bread that requires no butter, and is simply eaten as is. If you do desire some sort of lubrication, Liz suggests simply dipping the bread in saucers of extra-virgin olive oil.*

MAKES 2 LARGE
RECTANGULAR LOAVES

☞ INGREDIENTS

1 tablespoon of dry yeast
1/2 cup of warm water (not
    more than 115° F.) + 2 cups
    of additional warm water
1 tablespoon of sugar
1 tablespoon of salt
2 tablespoons of olive oil
5-7 cups of unbleached flour

TOPPING

2 tablespoons of extra-virgin
    olive oil
3 ripe summer tomatoes,
    peeled, seeded and chopped
    (or substitute 3 canned toma-
    toes, coarsely chopped)
12 Kalamata or other
    Mediterranean-style olives,
    pitted and chopped
24 2-inch sprigs of fresh rosemary
2 tablespoons of coarse sea salt
olive oil and cornmeal to coat
    baking sheets

SAGE FLAT BREAD

(1) Proof the yeast in the 1/2 cup of warm water in the bowl of a heavy duty mixer fitted with a dough hook.

(2) Add sugar and salt and stir to mix well.

(3) Add 2 remaining cups of warm water.

(4) Stir in whole wheat flour.

(5) Add 3 cups of all-purpose flour and the sage. Mix well and attach the dough hook to the mixer.

(6) Beat on low speed for 3 or 4 minutes.

(7) Increase speed and knead for another 5 minutes. If mixture is sticky, add some of remaining flour. Dough should clean the sides of the bowl and gather around the dough hook.

(8) Turn out into an oiled bowl.

(9) Turn to coat and cover with a clean towel.

(10) Put in a warm place to rise until doubled in bulk.

Preheat the oven to 400° F.

(11) Spray a cookie sheet with olive oil, Pam, or another non-stick spray.

(12) Coat with cornmeal.

(13) Spray the bottom of another sheet of equal size.

(14) Turn the dough out on a floured surface.

(15) Pat out into a circle and cut in fourths.

(16) Set 3 of the sections aside.

(17) With a rolling pin roll out the remaining section of dough to a thickness of 1/4-inch.

(18) Cut to fit cookie sheet.

(19) Sprinkle sea salt on surface of dough and press in gently. Top with other sheet.

(20) Place in preheated oven and bake for about 8 minutes.

(21) Remove top sheet and allow bread to slightly brown around the edges.

(22) Remove to a rack to cool.

(23) Repeat process with remaining dough, respraying and coating pans with cornmeal when necessary.

NOTE: *Break cooked bread into chunks and serve with sage and sun dried tomato butter.*

 INGREDIENTS

2 tablespoons of dry yeast
1/2 cup of warm water (not more than 115° F.)
1 tablespoon of sugar
1 tablespoon of salt
2 cups of warm water
2 cups of stone-ground whole wheat flour
3-5 cups of all-purpose flour
1/2 cup of chopped fresh sage
coarse sea salt
olive oil or non-stick spray for cookie sheet

MAKES ABOUT 100
ROUGHLY-BROKEN
CRACKERS

CHEDDAR AND CHILI
FLAT BREAD

(1) Proof yeast in 1/2 cup of warm water in the bowl of a heavy duty mixer fitted with a dough hook. (Lacking a mixer, proceed by hand as for any bread recipe.)

(2) Add sugar and salt and stir to mix well.

(3) Add 2 remaining cups of warm water.

(4) Stir in 5 to 6 cups of the all-purpose flour.

(5) Mix well and attach the dough hook to the mixer.

(6) Beat on low speed for 3 or 4 minutes.

(7) Increase speed and knead for another 5 minutes. If mixture is sticky, add some of the remaining flour. Dough should clean the sides of the bowl and gather around the dough hook.

(8) Divide dough in half.

(9) To one half, add 1 cup of shredded Cheddar cheese and 1 tablespoon of crumbled dried chili peppers.

Preheat the oven to 400° F.

(10) Spray a cookie sheet with olive oil, Pam, or other non-stick spray.

(11) Coat with cornmeal.

(12) Spray the bottom of another sheet of equal size.

(13) Turn the dough out on a floured surface.

(14) Pat out into a circle and cut in half.

(15) Set one of the sections aside.

(16) With a rolling pin, roll out the remaining section of dough to a thickness of 1/4-inch.

(17) Cut to fit cookie sheet.

(18) Sprinkle with sea salt on surface of dough and press in gently.

(19) Top with other sheet.

(20) Place in preheated oven and bake for about 8 minutes.

(21) Remove top sheet and slightly brown around the edges.

(22) Remove to a rack to cool.

(23) Repeat process with the remaining dough, respraying and coating pans with cornmeal when necessary.

HERBED ROUND LOAF

(1) Shape other half of dough into one round loaf. Allow to rise.
(2) Coat a 10-inch round cake pan with non-stick baking spray and sprinkle with cornmeal.
(3) Place dough in pan and allow to rise until doubled in bulk.
(4) Bake at 400° F. for 30 minutes or until loaf sounds hollow when tapped. Cool on a wire rack.
(5) With a serrated knife, slice loaf into 12 wedges.
(6) Spread with Herb Butter and reshape loaf. Wrap in foil.
(7) Heat foil-wrapped loaf in a 300° F. oven for 30 minutes before serving.

☞ INGREDIENTS

1 tablespoon of dry yeast
1/2 cup of warm water (not more than 115° F.)
1 tablespoon of sea salt
1 tablespoon of sugar
2 cups of warm water
5-8 cups of unbleached flour
1 cup of shredded Cheddar cheese
1 tablespoon of crumbled dried chili peppers
cornmeal and olive oil or non-stick spray for cookie sheets

HERB BUTTER

1 cup of lightly salted butter, softened at room temperature
1 tablespoon of poultry seasoning
2 large garlic cloves, peeled and mashed with a fork with 1 teaspoon of salt
1/2 cup of grated Parmesan cheese

(1) Cream all ingredients together.
(2) Spread between the wedges of the round loaf of bread.
(3) Use any remaining butter to coat the top of the loaf.

ROSEMARY FLAT BREAD

(1) Proof the yeast in the 1/2 cup of warm water in the bowl of a heavy duty mixer fitted with a dough hook. (Lacking a mixer, proceed by hand as for any bread recipe).

(2) Add sugar and salt and stir to mix well.

(3) Add the 2 remaining cups of warm water.

(4) Stir in whole wheat flour.

(5) Add 3 cups of all-purpose flour and the rosemary.

(6) Mix well and attach the dough hook to the mixer.

(7) Beat on low speed for 3 or 4 minutes.

(8) Increase speed and knead for another 5 minutes. If mixture is sticky, add some of remaining flour. Dough should clean the sides of the bowl and gather around the dough hook.

(9) Turn out into an oiled bowl.

(10) Turn to coat and cover with a clean towel.

(11) Put in a warm place to rise until doubled in bulk.

Preheat the oven to 400° F.

(12) Spray a cookie sheet with olive oil, Pam, or another non-stick spray.

(13) Coat with cornmeal.

(14) Spray the bottom of another sheet of equal size.

(15) Turn the dough out on a floured surface.

(16) Pat out into a circle and cut in fourths.

(17) Set 3 of the sections aside.

(18) With a rolling pin roll out the remaining section of dough to a thickness of 1/4-inch.

(19) Cut to fit cookie sheet.

(20) Sprinkle sea salt on surface of dough and press in gently. Top with other sheet.

(21) Place in preheated oven and bake for about 8 minutes.

(22) Remove top sheet and slightly brown around the edges.

(23) Remove to a rack to cool. Repeat process with remaining dough, respraying and coating pans with cornmeal when necessary.

NOTE: Break cooked bread into chunks and serve with rosemary and sun-dried tomato butter.

⚘ INGREDIENTS

2 tablespoons of dry yeast
1/2 cup of warm water (not more than 115° F.)
1 tablespoon of sugar
1 tablespoon of salt
2 cups of warm water
2 cups of stone-ground whole wheat flour
3-5 cups of all-purpose flour
1/2 cup of chopped fresh rosemary
coarse sea salt
olive oil or non-stick spray for cookie sheets

MAKES ABOUT 100 ROUGHLY-BROKEN CRACKERS

CARAWAY FLAT BREAD

(1) Proof the yeast in the 1/2 cup of warm water in the bowl of a heavy duty mixer fitted with a dough hook. (Lacking a mixer, proceed by hand as for any bread recipe).

(2) Add sugar and salt and stir to mix well.

(3) Add 2 remaining cups of warm water.

(4) Stir in whole wheat flour.

(5) Add 3 cups of all-purpose flour and the caraway seed.

(6) Mix well and attach the dough hook to the mixer.

(7) Beat on low speed for 3 or 4 minutes.

(8) Increase speed and knead for another 5 minutes. If mixture is sticky, add some of remaining flour. Dough should clean the sides of the bowl and gather around the dough hook.

(9) Turn out into an oiled bowl.

(10) Turn to coat and cover with a clean towel.

(11) Put in a warm place to rise until doubled in bulk.

Preheat the oven to 400° F.

(12) Spray a cookie sheet with olive oil, Pam, or another non-stick spray.

(13) Coat with cornmeal. Spray the bottom of another sheet of equal size.

(14) Turn the dough out on a floured surface.

(15) Pat out into a circle and cut in fourths.

(16) Set 3 of the sections aside.

(17) With a rolling pin roll out the remaining section of dough to a thickness of 1/4-inch.

(18) Cut to fit cookie sheet.

(19) Sprinkle sea salt on surface of dough and press in gently. Top with other sheet.

(20) Place in preheated oven and bake for about 8 minutes.

(21) Remove top sheet and slightly brown around the edges.

(22) Remove to a rack to cool.

(23) Repeat process with remaining dough, respraying and coating pans with cornmeal when necessary.

✿ INGREDIENTS

2 tablespoons of dry yeast
1/2 cup of warm water (not more
  than 115° F.)
1 tablespoon of sugar
1 tablespoon of salt
2 cups of warm water
2 cups of stone-ground whole wheat
  flour*
3-5 cups of all-purpose flour
3 tablespoons of caraway seed
coarse sea salt
olive oil or non-stick spray for cookie sheet

*Substitute rye flour if desired.

NOTE: *Break cooked bread into chunks and
serve with Anne Smith's Hot Bean Dip.*

MAKES ABOUT 100 ROUGHLY-BROKEN CRACKERS

ANNE SMITH'S HOT BEAN DIP

NOTE: *Liz's first memory of this dip
was a comment by her father on a
Christmas Eve party, saying to her
mother, "Honey, you have to get
Anne Smith's bean dip recipe!" Thirty
years later, here it is for you!
Deliciously different from most "ditzy"
sour cream and "salad dressing packet" dips, this is a hearty crowd-pleaser.
It reheats well—if there is any left!*

✿ INGREDIENTS

1 16-ounze can of kidney beans
1 cup of butter
1/2 pound of sharp cheese, grated
2 bottled hot peppers (chopped fine
  and 1 teaspoon of juice)
1 medium onion, grated
2 gloves garlic, minced

(1) Force beans thru a food mill.
(2) Mix ingredients in top of a double boiler.
(3) Heat until blended.
(4) Serve warm with assorted crackers.

HERBED FOUGASSE

(1) Proof yeast in 1/2 cup of warm water.
(2) Add the two remaining cups of warm water, salt, sugar, olive oil, and 5 cups of flour.
(3) Mix thoroughly.
(4) Add additional flour if dough is sticky. When a workable dough is achieved, knead until smooth and elastic (approximately 15 minutes by hand, or until the dough cleans the sides of the bowl if using a mixer with a dough hook).
(5) Brush a large bowl with olive oil. Place dough in bowl and turn to coat.
(6) Cover with a cloth and allow to rise until doubled in bulk.
(7) Turn dough out on a floured surface. Divide in half. Roll each half out in a rectangle.

(8) Cut slashes in a fan-like pattern completely through the loaves.
(9) Oil 2 large baking sheets and place dough on pans, opening the slashes on each loaf.
(10) Brush with olive oil.
(11) Sprinkle with sea salt and insert rosemary in a random pattern all over each loaf.

Preheat the oven to 400° F.

(12) Bake fougasse on center shelves of oven for 25 minutes, reversing pans after 15 minutes.
(13) Bake until loaves are golden and sound hollow when tapped. Cool on racks and break into pieces to serve.

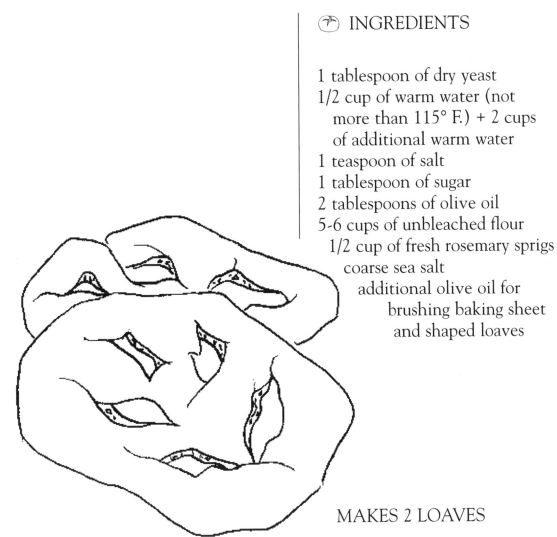

🐦 INGREDIENTS

1 tablespoon of dry yeast
1/2 cup of warm water (not
    more than 115° F.) + 2 cups
    of additional warm water
1 teaspoon of salt
1 tablespoon of sugar
2 tablespoons of olive oil
5-6 cups of unbleached flour
  1/2 cup of fresh rosemary sprigs
    coarse sea salt
      additional olive oil for
        brushing baking sheet
        and shaped loaves

MAKES 2 LOAVES

FOUGASSE SUCRE
SUGARED FOUGASSE

(1) Proof yeast in 1/2 cup of warm water.

(2) Add the two remaining cups of warm water, salt, sugar, orange flower water, olive oil, and 5 cups of flour. Mix thoroughly.

(3) Add additional flour if dough is sticky.

(4) When a workable dough is achieved, knead until smooth and elastic (approximately 15 minutes by hand, or until the dough cleans the sides of the bowl if using a mixer with a dough hook.

(5) Brush a large bowl with olive oil.

(6) Place dough in oiled bowl and turn to coat.

(7) Cover with a cloth and allow to rise until doubled in bulk.

(8) Turn dough out on a floured surface.

(9) Divide in half. Roll each half out into a rectangle.

(10) Cut slashes in a fan-like pattern completely through the loaves.

(11) Oil 2 large baking sheets and place dough on pans opening the slashes on each loaf.

(12) Brush with egg wash (1 egg + 1 tablespoon water, whisked.)

(13) Sprinkle with Parle Sucre or pearl sugar–available from specialty bakeries or the King Arthur Flour Catalog**

Preheat the oven to 400° F.

(14) Place the baking pan with the loaves on the center shelf of the preheated oven.

(15) Bake for 25-30 minutes, or until loaves are golden and sounds hollow when tapped. Remove from oven and cool loaves on a baking rack.

** King Arthur Flour
P O Box 1010
Norwich, VT 05055

NOTE: *"Tomorrow's the festival of the Kings. This evening they arrive. If you want to see them, little ones, go quickly to meet them—and take presents for them, and for their pages, and for the poor camels who have come so far!" (Mistral) The traditional Christmas bread of Provence. Mistral describes running down the road toward Arles, waiting for the Kings to pass, carrying "fougasso" for the Kings, figs for the pages, and hay for the "poor tired camels who have come so far."*

☞ INGREDIENTS

1 tablespoon of dry yeast
1/2 cup of warm water (not more than 115° F.)
2 cups of warm water (not more than 115° F.)
6 tablespoons of sugar
3 tablespoons of orange flower water*
2 tablespoons of olive oil
5-6 cups of unbleached flour
1 egg + 1 tablespoon water
Parle Sucre (pearl sugar)

*Orange flower water is available in most oriental markets.

MAKES 2 LOAVES

BACON FOUGASSE

(1) In a large heavy bottomed skillet, fry bacon until crisp.

(2) Remove bacon to paper towels to drain.

(3) Reserve 4 tablespoons of the bacon fat, plus 2 tablespoons for final glazing.

(4) Proof yeast in 1/2 cup of warm water with the sugar.

(5) Add the two remaining cups of warm water, reserved bacon fat and 5 cups of flour. Mix thoroughly.

(6) Add more flour if dough is sticky. When a workable dough is achieved, knead until smooth and elastic. (Approximately 15 minutes by hand, or until the mixture forms a ball and cleans the sides of the bowl, if using a mixer with a dough hook.)

(7) Knead in the crisp bacon.

(8) Brush a large bowl with oil, place dough in bowl and turn to coat.

(9) Cover bowl with a linen towel and place in a warm place to rise until doubled in bulk.

(10) Turn dough out on a floured surface and pat into a circle.

(11) Divide in half. Roll each half into a rectangle.

(12) Cut slashes in the dough with a sharp knife in a fan-shaped pattern, cutting through the dough.

(13) Spray 2 large baking sheets with non-stick spray.

(14) Sprinkle with cornmeal.

(15) Place dough on baking sheets and open the slits, tucking back the edges so that they do not close as the dough rises.

Preheat the oven to 400° F.

(16) Brush loaves with a little of the remaining bacon fat.

(17) Bake fougasse on center shelves of the preheated oven for 30 minutes, reversing the pans after 15 minutes.
(18) Loaves should be golden and sound hollow when tapped. Cool on racks and break into pieces to serve.

NOTE: *Liz first encountered this Bacon Fougasse, or "Fougasse Salé" when she made an early morning excursion to a local bakery with host David Carpita in St. Remy de Provence. The bakers, in sandals and swim trunks, slid the breads in and out of wood-fired ovens on long-handled paddles. Obviously not overrun with tourists, unlike the famous bakeries of Paris, they grinned and eagerly volunteered to pose for Liz's camera!*

☞ INGREDIENTS

1 pound slab of bacon, cut into 1/2x1/4-inch pieces
1 tablespoon of dry yeast
1/2 cup of warm water (not more than 115° F.)
2 cups of warm water (not more than 115° F.)
1 tablespoon of sugar
1 tablespoon of salt
5-6 cups of unbleached flour
non-stick spray for coating baking sheets
cornmeal for sprinkling sheets

MAKES 2 LOAVES

DRIED APPLE, ROSEMARY
FOUGASSE

(1) Proof yeast in 1/2 cup of warm apple liquid with the tablespoon of sugar.

(2) Add the two remaining cups of liquid and the salt. Whisk thoroughly to combine.

(3) Add 5 cups of the flour. Mix thoroughly.

(4) Add the drained, diced apples.

(5) Add more flour if dough is sticky. When a workable dough is achieved, knead until smooth and elastic. (Approximately 15 minutes by hand, or until the mixture forms a ball and cleans the sides of the bowl, if using a mixer with a dough hook.)

(6) Brush a large bowl with oil, place dough in bowl and turn to coat.

(7) Cover bowl with a linen towel and place in a warm place to rise until doubled in bulk.

(8) Turn dough out on a floured surface and pat into a circle.

(9) Divide in half. Roll each half into a large fan shape.

(10) Cut slashes in the dough echoing the fan shape.

(11) Tuck dough under to open each slash.

(12) Coat 2 large baking sheets with olive oil.

(13) Place dough on sheets making sure that slits remain open.

(14) Stick sprigs of rosemary in a loose pattern across the loaf.

(15) Sprinkle with sea salt and brush loaves lightly with olive oil.

Preheat the oven to 400° F.

(16) Bake fougasse on center shelves of the preheated oven for 30 minutes, reversing the loaves after 15 minutes.

(17) Leaves should sound hollow when tapped. Cool on racks. Break into pieces to serve.

NOTE: *This is Liz's appled-up version of the classic large, lacy loaves of Provence. Sweet and savory versions of this bread are found throughout the Mediterranean regions of southern France. This fresh-tasting loaf, great for an accompaniment to soup, can be easily made if you keep a pot of fresh rosemary on hand and dried apples in the cupboard.*

☞ INGREDIENTS

1-ounce package of dried apples, diced, covered with water and simmered briefly to reconstitute, drained, and liquid reserved

1 tablespoon of dry yeast

1/2 cup of warm (not more than 115° F.) liquid drained from the reconstituted apples

2 cups of warm (not more than 115° F.) liquid drained from the reconstituted apples

1 tablespoon of sugar

1 tablespoon of sea salt

5-6 cups of unbleached flour

12-15 sprigs of fresh rosemary (1-inch long)

sea salt for sprinkling loaves

olive oil for coating leaves and baking sheets

MAKES 2 LOAVES

FRESH CORN, CORNMEAL, ROSEMARY
FLAT BREAD

(1) In the bowl of a heavy duty mixer fitted with the dough hook, whisk together the 1/2 cup water, the yeast and the sugar.

(2) Allow to stand until foamy.

(3) Add the reserved softened corn-meal, the sea salt and the 2 remaining cups of warm water. Whisk to combine.

(4) Begin adding the all-purpose flour to the mixture until a dough is formed.

(5) Place the bowl on the mixer and knead on medium-high until the dough begins to form gluten strands which stretch from the sides of the bowl. (This is not a dough which you want to clean the sides of the bowl. It should remain fairly wet.)

(6) Stir in the cut corn kernels and the rosemary.

(7) Oil a large plastic or ceramic mixing bowl with the vegetable oil and turn the dough out into the bowl.

(8) Turn to coat the top of the dough with oil.

(9) Cover with a clean cotton or linen dish cloth and set aside to rise until the dough doubles in bulk.

(10) Turn the dough out onto a floured cloth and pat out into a circle about 1-inch thick.

(11) With a sharp knife cut the circle into four equal pieces.

(12) With a rolling pin, roll out each circle until it is about 1/4-inch thick.

Preheat the oven to 400° F.

(13) Spray one cookie sheet for each loaf with non-stick spray.* Sprinkle with cornmeal.

(14) Spray the bottom of another sheet and place the other sheet on top of it.

(15) Place in the preheated oven for 10 minutes.

(16) Remove the top sheet and continue to bake until the bread is golden and crisp around the edges.

(17) Remove from oven and cool on racks. Break into pieces when cool.

* Unless you have a battery of baking sheets you will have to bake this bread in batches, cooling the sheets each time.

NOTE: This sweet, slightly crispy bread is a perfect accompaniment to any number of summer soups. Make it during the height of sweet corn season when you are buying dozens of ears inexpensively at your farmer's markets and roadside stands. Be sure to plan far enough ahead to soak your cornmeal in boiling water to soften. (Two hours ahead, or even over-night is just fine.) If you are fond of southwestern flavors, chopped chilies are a great addition to this bread.

✍ INGREDIENTS

2 cups of preferably stone-ground cornmeal (covered with 1 cup of boiling water and mixed thoroughly, then allowed to cool and stand for at least 2 hours), reserved
1/2 cup of warm water (not more than 115° F.)
1 tablespoon of active dry yeast
1 tablespoon of sugar
1 tablespoon of sea salt
2 cups of warm water (not more than 115° F.)
5-7 cups of all-purpose flour
kernels cut from 2 medium ears of fresh sweet corn (about 3/4-cup)
3 tablespoons of chopped fresh rosemary
vegetable oil for oiling bowl
non-stick spray and cornmeal for baking sheets

MAKES 4 FLAT LOAVES

TARTE FLAMBÉE

(1) Prepare the dough for French Loaves (keep the dough fairly wet).

(2) After the first rise, divide dough into thirds.

(3) Shape the remaining 2/3's of dough into baguettes and bake according to the directions in the Baguette recipe, or multiply the filling to make 3 tartes.

(4) Sauté the bacon until it renders its fat.

(5) Remove the bacon with a slotted spoon and reserve.

(6) Sauté the onions in the bacon fat until they are transparent.

(7) Return bacon to the pan and cook mixture until you can touch the bottom of the pan.

(8) Spray an 11x14-inch baking sheet with sides with non-stick spray.

(9) Roll out 1/3 of the bread dough on a floured surface.

(10) Cut the dough to fit the baking sheet.

(11) Pinch the sides of the dough to form a rim around the tarte.

Preheat the oven to 400° F.

(12) Spread sautéed onions and bacon over tarte.

(13) Carefully pour cream over tarte's surface.

(14) Grate nutmeg, salt, and pepper across the top.

(15) Place the tarte on the center shelf of the preheated oven.

(16) Bake for 25–30 minutes, or until sides of tarte are quite brown and most of the cream has evaporated and thickened.

(17) Cut with a pizza wheel and serve warm.

✿ INGREDIENTS

1 recipe of basic French loaves (see
    page 22, Rustic Baguettes)
1/2 pound of thick-sliced bacon,
    diced
2 large yellow onions, peeled and
    sliced
3/4–1 cup of heavy cream
freshly grated nutmeg
sea salt
freshly ground pepper
non-stick spray for baking sheets

NOTE: *This rich bread dough-based tarte might be termed "Alsatian Pizza." It makes a great accompaniment to a glass of wine and serves as a first course as well. Long time dinner regulars–Stephanie Klepfer and Jim Hoffman–have tasted a plethora of Liz's appetizers, but when she served this with their aperitif one chilly evening in front of the library fireplace, they pronounced it their "all-time favorite" from among her hors d'ourvres!*

SERVES 8

GOUGÈRES

Preheat the oven to 425° F.

(1) Line 2 baking sheets with parchment paper. Set aside.

(2) Bring the water and the butter to a boil in a heavy 2-quart saucepan over medium-high heat. The butter should melt as the water comes to a boil.

(3) Add the flour all at once.

(4) With a wooden spoon stir constantly until the mixture forms a ball around the spoon and cleans the sides of the pan. Continue to cook, stirring constantly for 3-4 minutes. (Flour must cook through to avoid a raw taste.)

(5) Place mixture in the container of a food processor*, fitted with the steel blade.

(6) With motor running, add eggs, one at a time, until all are incorporated.

(7) Add all remaining ingredients and process until combined.

(8) With a large rubber spatula place the dough in a pastry bag with a 1-inch plain tip. (Note: Lacking a pastry bag, use two spoons to lay out 1-inch mounds of dough on the parchment covered baking sheet.)

NOTE: *You should be able to pipe or spoon about 24 gougères on each sheet. Be sure to allow about an inch or more between mounds of dough, as they will expand dramatically.*

(9) Place one sheet at a time on the middle shelf of the preheated oven. Bake for 10-12 minutes, watching to see that the bottoms of the puffs do not brown too much. When gougères are puffed and golden, remove to a rack to cool.

* If you do not have a food processor, all ingredients may be stirred into the dough in the pan. You probably will only be able to incorporate 3 of the eggs, however.

NOTE: *A classic Burgundian hors d'oeuvres, Liz has eaten these as an amuse-gueule in such stellar restaurants as Taillevent and George Blanc. In 1994, she happened to be in Beaune, the wine center of Burgundy, on he 4th of July. The mayor of Beaune invited her to an Independence Day Celebration in the wine cellars of the Dukes of Burgundy, where good Burgundian wine, Kir, and gougères were served, as the American/French Connection was toasted. Make a batch of these cheese cream puffs, pour yourself a glass of good red wine, and toast the red, white and blue of both nations!*

INGREDIENTS

1 cup of cold water
8 tablespoons of butter
1 cup of unbleached flour
4 extra-large eggs
1 teaspoon of salt
1 teaspoon of dry mustard
dash of cayenne
1 cup of shredded Swiss cheese (Emmentaler or Gruyère preferred)

MAKES ABOUT 48 PUFFS

TRUFFLED BRIOCHE
THE HUNDRED DOLLAR LOAF

(1) In the bowl of a heavy duty mixer, fitted with the paddle attachment whisk together the water, yeast, and tablespoon of sugar. Allow to stand until foamy.

(2) Add the flour and the 1/2 cup of sugar and mix to combine.

(3) Add the eggs and the egg yolks and mix on medium speed until a very sticky dough forms. Add the softened butter and mix in completely. Stir in the truffles. This dough is extremely sticky and impossible to handle. Do not be alarmed.

(4) Brush a large plastic or ceramic bowl with vegetable oil, and using a spatula, (the hand-held French curved spatula called a corm is ideal for this), scrape the dough into the bowl, turn it, if possible, and cover the bowl with plastic wrap.

(5) Place the bowl in the refrigerator for at lest 6 hours, or overnight.

(6) Spray a 16x4x4-inch Pullman pan (Pullman pans are available from Bridge Kitchenware, 214 East 52nd Street, New York, NY 10022 212-688-4220, www.bridgekitchenware.com), or two 8x4-inch loaf pans with non-stick spray. (If using the Pullman pan all of the dough can be shaped into one loaf. If using the smaller loaf pans, divide dough in half.)

(7) While the dough is still cold, push it down and shape into one or two long cylinders, according to your pans.

(8) Place dough in the oiled pans and cover with a clean cloth. Allow to rise until dough has doubled in bulk. (Because the dough is cold, this may take anywhere from an hour to an hour and a half.)

Preheat the oven to 375° F.

(9) If using a Pullman pan, spray the inside of the lid and slide the lid onto the pan and place the pan in the middle of a shelf which has been centered in the oven. If using two loaf pans, spray the bottom of a light-colored cookie sheet large enough to cover both with the non-stick spray and place it over the loaf pans in the oven.

(10) Top the cookie sheet with a brick to prevent its being dislodged as the loaves rise.

(11) Bake for one hour. (Check the smaller loaves after 45 minutes.)

(12) Remove from oven and allow to cool in pans for a few minutes before turning out onto a cooling rack. Do not attempt to slice these loaves until they are completely cool. Slice thinly to serve.

NOTE: *This bread freezes extremely well.*

NOTE: *It is necessary to begin the dough the night before and allow it to rise over-night in the refrigerator, otherwise the dough is impossibly soft and cannot be shaped or handled.*

NOTE: *As Shirley Corriher said when Liz told her of this recipe—"Liz has taken brioche beyond the pale!" Shirley makes what she terms "The Ultimate Brioche," but Liz's addition of minced truffles to the rich, egg and butter dough makes this not only one of the richest, but one of the most extravagant breads imaginable.*

⁘ INGREDIENTS

1/2 cup of warm water (not more than 115° F.)

1 tablespoon of yeast

1 tablespoon of sugar

4 cups of all-purpose flour

1/2 cup of sugar

3 extra-large eggs

2 extra-large egg yolks

1 pound of lightly salted butter, softened

1/2 cup of canned black truffles, minced in a food processor, and reserved

vegetable oil for oiling bowl

non-stick spray for baking pan

MAKES 1 16-INCH OR 2 8-INCH LOAVES

EASY FOOD PROCESSOR CHEESE BRIOCHE

(1) Put 1/2 cup of warm water in the bowl of a food processor fitted with the steel blade.
(2) Add the yeast and allow to proof.
(3) Put the flour, sugar, cheese, and butter in the processor bowl and blend with a series of on/off turns until the mixture resembles cornmeal. Add the eggs and process until the dough strains the motor or the motor stops running.
(4) Remove dough from bowl and place in a greased mixing bowl.
(5) Cover with plastic wrap and let rise until doubled in bulk.
(6) Punch dough down and refrigerate overnight.
(7) At this point the dough may be used to shape the traditional brioche rolls or rolled out to form a crust. If making traditional brioche, place them in tins and allow to rise until doubled in size.
(8) Glaze with beaten egg and bake in a preheated 375° F. oven for 25 minutes, or until golden.

☞ INGREDIENTS

2 tablespoons of dry yeast
1/2 cup of warm water (not more than 115° F.)
4 1/2 cups of flour
1/2 cup of sugar
1 1/2 cups of cold butter (cut in pieces)
6 extra-large eggs
1 cup of grated cheese (Cheddar, Swiss, or Monterey Jack)

MAKES ABOUT 2 DOZEN BRIOCHE

HERBED FOUGASSE
BREAD MACHINE VERSION

(1) Place ingredients, in order given, in pan of bread machine. Set machine on BREAD and FIRST RISE and start.

(2) When machine beeps, signaling completion of first rise, turn dough out on to floured surface.

(3) Roll out into a rectangle.

(4) Cut slashes in a fan-like pattern completely through the loaf.

(5) Oil a large baking sheet and place dough on pan, opening the slashes on the loaf.

(6) Brush with olive oil.

(7) Sprinkle with sea salt and insert rosemary in a random pattern all over loaf.

(8) Cover loosely with plastic wrap and let rise until doubled.

Preheat the oven to 400° F.

(9) Bake fougasse for about 25 minutes until golden. Cool on rack and break into pieces to serve.

INGREDIENTS

1 1/8 cups of water
1 tablespoon of olive oil
3 cups of unbleached flour
1 1/2 teaspoons of salt
1 1/2 teaspoons of sugar
1 1/2 teaspoons of Red Star yeast
1/4 cup fresh rosemary sprigs
coarse sea salt
additional olive oil for brushing
    pan and loaf

NOTE: This recipe was prepared in a Hitachi bread machine and may need minor adjustments for some other brands of machine.

MAKES 1 LOAF

BRAIDED SWEET POTATO BREAD
BREAD MACHINE VERSION

(1) Place ingredients, in order given, in pan of bread machine.

(2) Set machine on BREAD and FIRST RISE and start.

(3) When machine beeps, signaling completion of first rise turn dough out on to floured board.

(4) Knead a minute or two, then cover and let rest for 10 minutes.

(5) Spray a large baking sheet with non-stick spray coating; sprinkle with cornmeal.

(6) Pat dough into a circle about 1-inch thick.

(7) With a sharp knife, cut dough into three equal wedges.

(8) With floured hands roll the wedges from wide end into cylinders and stretch into even ropes about 16 inches long.

(9) Braid the three ropes by crossing them in the middle and braiding toward each end.

(10) Tuck the ends under; press to seal.

(11) Place the braid diagonally on the prepared baking sheet.

(12) Cover and let rise in a warm place until doubled.

Preheat the oven to 400 °F.

(13) Combine egg and 1 tablespoon of water.

(14) Brush braid with egg mixture.

(15) Sprinkle with 1 1/2 teaspoons caraway seed.

(16) Bake at 400° F. degrees for about 35 minutes until loaf is golden and sounds hollow when tapped

(17) Remove from oven, remove loaf from baking sheet and cool on wire rack.

NOTE: *This recipe was prepared in a Hitachi bread machine and may need minor adjustments for some other brands of machine.*

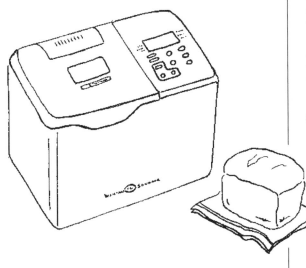

🐦 INGREDIENTS

1 1/8 cups of water
1 cup of mashed yam, cooled
2 1/4 cups of bread flour
1/2 cup of stone-ground rye flour
1/4 cup of stone-ground whole
  wheat flour
1 1/2 teaspoons of sugar
1 1/2 teaspoons of sea salt or
  regular salt
1 1/2 teaspoons of caraway seed
1 1/2 teaspoons of Red Star yeast

additional ingredients for steps 5 through 15: (The ingredients listed above are for step 1.)
  non-stick spray coating
  cornmeal
  1 egg
  1 tablespoon of water
1 1/2 teaspoons of caraway seed

MAKES 1 LOAF

BARLEY AND ONION COUNTRY LOAF
BREAD MACHINE VERSION

(1) Place ingredients, in order given, in pan of bread machine.

(2) Set machine on BREAD and FIRST RISE and start.

(3) When machine beeps, signaling completion of first rise, turn dough out onto floured surface and pat out into a circle about 1-inch thick.

(4) Form into a round loaf by rolling sides in and pinching together.

(5) Coat top with flour and place, pinched-side down, on a cookie sheet which has been greased and coated with cornmeal.

(6) Cover loaf with linen towel and allow to rise for about an hour.

Preheat the oven to 400° F.

(7) Slash top of loaf.

(8) Place loaf in oven and bake for about 30 minutes, until it sounds hollow when tapped. Cool on rack.

☞ INGREDIENTS

1 1/8 cups of water

1 medium yellow onion, peeled and diced

1/2 cup of prepared quick-cooking barley

1 cup of stone-ground whole wheat flour

2 cups of bread flour

1 1/2 teaspoons of sugar

1 1/2 teaspoons of salt

1 1/2 teaspoons of Red Star yeast

NOTE: *This recipe was prepared in a Hitachi bread machine and may need minor adjustments for some other brands of machine.*

MAKES 1 LOAF

HONEY, SUNFLOWER SEED & CRACKED WHEAT LOAF
BREAD MACHINE VERSION

(1) Place ingredients, in order given, in pan of bread machine.

(2) Set machine on BREAD and FIRST RISE and start.

(3) When machine beeps, signaling completion of first rise, turn dough out on to floured surface, pat out and cut into two pieces.

(4) Roll sides in and pinch together, forming round loaves.

(5) Place loaves, pinched-side down on cookie sheets which have been greased and coated with cornmeal. Cover.

(6) Allow to rise for about an hour.

Preheat the oven to 400° F.

(7) Slash tops of loaves.

(8) Bake for 30 minutes, until loaves sound hollow when tapped.

NOTE: *This recipe was prepared in a Hitachi bread machine and may need minor adjustments for some other brands of machine.*

INGREDIENTS

1 1/4 cups of water

1 Tablespoon of olive oil

1 Tablespoon of honey

1/4 cup cracked wheat cereal soaked in l/2 cup boiling water and cooled

1 1/2 cups of stone-ground whole wheat flour

1 1/2 cups of bread flour

1 1/2 teaspoons of salt

l/2 cup of roasted, hulled sunflower seeds

2 teaspoons of Red Star yeast

MAKES 2 LOAVES

INDEX

Traditional Country Life Recipe Books from
BRICK TOWER PRESS

Forthcoming titles:

Sandwich Companion
Cranberry Companion
Farmstand Companion
Pie Companion

Other titles in this series:

American Chef's Companion
Chocolate Companion
Fresh Herb Companion
Thanksgiving Cookery
Victorian Christmas Cookery
Apple Companion
Pumpkin Companion
Soups, Stews & Chowders

Liz Clark teaches cooking in her restored antebellum home on the bluffs above the Mississippi River in historic Keokuk, Iowa. To request a newsletter of her upcoming classes, call Southeastern Community College at 1-319-752-2731. (E-mail: sseabold@secc.cc.ia.us) Web: www.secc.cc.ia.us (Continuing Education)

MAIL ORDER AND GENERAL INFORMATION
Many of our titles are carried by your local book store or gift and museum shop. If they do not already carry our line please ask them to write us for information.

If you are unable to purchase our titles from your local shop, call or write to us.
Our titles are available through mail order. Just send us a check or money order for $9.95 per title with $1.50 postage (shipping is free with 3 or more assorted copies) to the address below or call us Monday through Friday, 9 AM to 5PM, EST. We accept Visa, Mastercard, and American Express.

Send all mail order, book club, and special sales requests to the address below or call us for a free catalog. We can mail our catalog to you or e-mail a paperfree copy. In any case we would like to hear from you.

Brick Tower Press (US)
1230 Park Avenue
New York, NY 10128
www.bricktowerpress.com

Brick Tower Press (UK)
52 Parkwood Road
Wimborne, Dorset BH21 1LG
www.podpub.co.uk

Telephone & Facsimile
1-212-427-7139
1-800-68-BRICK

Telephone & Facsimile
(01202) 889362

E-mail
bricktower@aol.com

E-mail
norman@podpub.freeserve.co.uk